THE PENGUIN P

THE PENGUIN
OF CANADIAN VERSE

The Penguin Book of CANADIAN VERSE

Fourth Revised Edition

EDITED WITH AN
INTRODUCTION AND NOTES BY
Ralph Gustafson

PENGUIN BOOKS

Penguin Books Ltd, Harmondsworth, Middlesex, England
Penguin Books, 40 West 23rd Street, New York, New York 10010, U.S.A.
Penguin Books Australia Ltd, Ringwood, Victoria, Australia
Penguin Books Canada Ltd, 2801 John Street, Markham, Ontario, Canada L3R 1B4
Penguin Books (N.Z.) Ltd, 182–190 Wairau Road, Auckland 10, New Zealand

Published in Pelican Books 1942, as
The Pelican Anthology of Canadian Poetry
Published in Penguin Books 1958
Revised edition 1967
Reprinted 1971, 1972
Revised edition 1975
Reprinted 1977, 1980
Revised edition 1984

—

—

The Acknowledgements on pp. 19–23 constitute an
extension of this copyright page

—

Manufactured in U.K. by
Cox & Wyman Ltd, Reading

—

CANADIAN CATALOGUING IN PUBLICATION DATA

Main entry under title:
Penguin book of Canadian verse

Includes index.
ISBN 0-14-042329-X

1. Canadian poetry (English). I. Gustafson, Ralph,
1909– II. Title: Canadian verse.

PS8273.P4 1984 C811'.008 C83-098754-1
PR9195.23.P4 1984

TO THE MEMORY OF

E. J. PRATT

Contents

Acknowledgements

PERMISSION to use copyright material is gratefully acknowledged to the following:

Behrman House, Inc., New York, for 'Heirloom' and 'The Still Small Voice' from *Hath not a Jew . . .* by A. M. Klein.

Chatto & Windus Ltd, London, for the poems from *The Wounded Prince* and *The Net and the Sword* by Douglas Le Pan; and *Lyric XCIII* from *Sappho, One Hundred Lyrics* by Bliss Carman.

Clarke, Irwin & Company Ltd, Toronto, for 'Romance' from *In Search of Eros* by Elizabeth Brewster.

Coach House Press, Toronto, for 'Song to Alfred Hitchcock and Wilkinson' from *The Dainty Monsters*, 'White Dwarfs' and 'We're at the graveyard' from *Rat Jelly* by Michael Ondaatje.

Dodd, Mead & Company Inc., New York, for 'Low Tide on Grand Pré', 'A Northern Vigil', 'A Seamark', and 'Christmas Song', by Bliss Carman, reprinted by permission of Dodd, Mead & Company from *Bliss Carman's Poems*.

Estate of Frederick George Scott for the poems by Frederick George Scott.

House of Anansi Press, Toronto, for 'They Are Hostile Nations' from *Power Politics* by Margaret Atwood; two sections from *The Happy Hungry Man* by George Jonas; 'Wild Horses' and 'Bunkhouse North' from *Beware the Months of Fire* by Patrick Lane; 'Coming Back' and 'Horse' from *At the Edge of the Chopping There Are No Secrets* by John Thompson.

Jewish Publication Society of America, Philadelphia, for 'Psalms VI and XII' from *Poems* by A. M. Klein.

Alfred A. Knopf, Inc., New York, for the poems of E. J. Pratt, reprinted from *Collected Poems*, copyright 1945 by Edward J. Pratt.

McClelland & Stewart Limited, Toronto, 'Shrouds and Away' from *Border River* by A. G. Bailey; selections from *Selected Poems* by Earle Birney; selections from *Bliss Carman's Poems*; selections from *The Spice-Box of Earth* and *Flowers for Hitler* by Leonard Cohen; 'Jardin de la Chapelle Expiatoire' from *The Strength of the Hills* by Robert Finch; 'Utrillo's World' from *The Deficit Made Flesh* by John Glassco; selections from *Collected Poems* by Irving Layton; 'White Lies' from *Lies* by John Newlove; 'Summer' from *The Metal and the Flower* by P. K. Page; selections from *The Complete Poems of Marjorie Pickthall*; 'At Delos' from *The Circle of Affection* by Duncan Campbell Scott; 'Goat' and 'Eagle' from *Timelight* by Robin Skelton; 'Picketing Supermarkets', 'Unemployment', and 'Wayman in Love' from *Waiting for Wayman* by Tom Wayman.

The Macmillan Company of Canada Ltd, Toronto, for 'The Child Dancing' from *The Armies of the Moon* by Gwendolyn MacEwen; selection from *A Suit of Nettles* by James Reaney; selections from *Collected Poems* by E. J. Pratt; 'Lens' and 'In June and Gentle Oven' from *The Hangman Ties the Holly* by Anne Wilkinson. 'A Cautionary Tale' and excerpts from 'Nature Be Damned' reprinted by permission of the estate of Anne Wilkinson and The Macmillan Company of Canada Limited.

Michigan State University Press for 'Ode: On the Death of William Butler Yeats', 'The Plot against Proteus', and 'The Archer' from *A Sort of Ecstasy* by A. J. M. Smith.

The New Yorker Magazine, Inc., for 'From a Journal' by George Amabile © 1973; and for 'War on the Periphery' by George Johnston © 1951; reprinted by permission of The New Yorker Magazine, Inc.

W. W. Norton & Company Inc., New York, for '. . . Person, or A Hymn on and to the Holy Ghost', 'For Dr and Mrs Dresser', and 'Janitor Working on Threshold' from *The Dumbfounding* by Margaret Avison © 1966 by Margaret Avison.

Oberon Press, Ottawa, for 'To Dona Isabel, Protectress of the Faith' and 'Virgin' from *Catalan Poems* by George McWhirter: reprinted by permission of Oberon Press.

Oxford University Press, Toronto, for 'Notes from Various Pasts' from *The Animals in that Country* by Margaret Atwood; 'The Statue' from *Poems* by Robert Finch; 'Quebec Farmhouse' and 'Brummell at Calais' from *A Point of Sky* by John Glassco; 'Music in the Air' from *Home Free* by George Johnston; 'The Swan' and 'The Fisherman' from *The Boatman* by Jay Macpherson; 'News of the Phoenix', and 'The Sorcerer' from *Collected Poems* by A. J. M. Smith.

L. C. Page & Company, Boston, for selections from *Poems* by Charles G. D. Roberts; and 'Lyric XCIII' from *Sappho* by Bliss Carman: reprinted by permission of the copyright owner, L. C. Page & Company, Boston.

Press Porcepic, Erin, Ont., for 'All Worlds Lead to the Lobe' from *Dream Craters* and 'The Spider' from *Bumblebee Dithyramb* by Joe Rosenblatt.

Proprietors of *Punch* for 'In Flanders Fields' by John McCrae, reproduced by permission of *Punch*.

The Ryerson Press, Toronto, for 'Cold Colloquy' from *The White Centre* by Patrick Anderson; 'Bushed' from *Trial of a City* by Earle Birney; 'How One Winter Came in the Lake Region' from *The Collected Poems of Wilfred Campbell*; 'The Pomegranate' from *The Searching Image* by Louis Dudek; 'Roadside near Moscow' from *A Window on the North* by R. A. D. Ford; 'Haying' from *Marshlands* by John Frederic Herbin; 'The Rocking Chair' and 'Bread' from *The Rocking Chair* by A. M. Klein; selections from *Collected Poems of Raymond Knister*; two sonnets from *By Stubborn Stars* by Kenneth Leslie; 'The Thing is Violent' from *A Breakfast for Barbarians* by Gwendolyn MacEwen; 'Zalinka' from *Complete Poems of Tom MacInnes*; 'David' from *Black and Secret Man* by Eli Mandel; selections from *Selected Poems of Sir Charles G. D. Roberts*; 'The Blue Heron' and 'The Wreckers' Prayer' from *The Leather Bottle* by Theodore Goodridge Roberts; 'The Piper of Arll', 'Thoughts', 'Watkwenies', 'The Onondaga

Madonna', 'The Sailor's Sweetheart', 'A Song' from *The Selected Poems of Duncan Campbell Scott*; 'A Grain of Rice', 'Caring', 'Bonne Entente' from *Events and Signals* by F. R. Scott; 'The Yak' and 'Exile' from *Leaves in the Wind* by Virna Sheard; 'Ode: On the Death of William Butler Yeats', 'The Plot against Proteus', 'The Archer' from *A Sort of Ecstasy* by A. J. M. Smith; 'The Six-quart Basket' and 'Where the Blue Horses' from *The Colour of the Times* by Raymond Souster; 'Thou Didst Say Me' from *The Second Silence* and 'The Season's Lovers' from *The Season's Lovers* by Miriam Waddington.

The University of New Brunswick for permission for world rights outside Canada and U.S.A. to reprint the selections from the poems of Bliss Carman.

Mrs B. H. Warr for the poems by Bertram Warr.

University of Toronto Press for 'Northern Water Thrush' from *The Sun is Axeman* by D. G. Jones.

Grateful acknowledgement is made to the following authors: Margaret Avison for her poems; George Bowering for his poems from *The Silver Wire* (Contact Press); Louis Dudek for 'Dawn' from *Twenty Four Poems*, selections from *Europe*, 'The Jungle' and 'Mouths' from *The Transparent Sea* (Contact Press); R. G. Everson for 'Child with Shell' and 'When I'm Going Well' from *A Lattice for Momos* (Contact Press) and 'Rogue Pearunners' from *Wrestle with an Angel* (Delta Canada); Marya Fiamengo for her poems; Eldon Grier for 'Quebec' from *A Morning from Scraps*, 'In Memory of Garcia Lorca' from *Poems*, 'On the Subject of Waves' and 'View from a Window' from *A Friction of Lights* (Contact Press); D. G. Jones for 'Annunciation'; Lionel Kearns for 'In-Group' and 'Insight'; Leo Kennedy for his poems; Irving Layton for his poems from *The Improved Binoculars*; Malcolm Lowry for his poems; Pat Lowther for her poems from *This Difficult Flowering* (Very Stone House, Vancouver); Eli Mandel for 'Phaeton' from *Fuseli Poems* (Contact Press); Tom Marshall for 'Astrology' from *The Beast with Three Backs* (Quarry Press); Seymour Mayne for his poems; John Newlove for 'I Talk to You' and 'Good Company, Fine Houses' from *Moving in Alone* (Contact Press); Alden Nowlan for 'God Sour the Milk of the Knacking Wench' from *Wind in a Rocky Country* (Emblem Book), 'The Execution' from *The Things Which Are* (Contact Press); Alfred Purdy for 'Wilderness Gothic' and 'The Sculptors'; P. K. Page for poems from *As Ten as Twenty*; W. W. E. Ross for his poems; F. R. Scott for 'Calamity'; David Solway for 'The Last Supper' from *The Egyptian Airforce* (Fiddlehead Poetry Books); Raymond Souster for 'Flight of the Roller-Coaster' from *The Selected Poems* (Contact Press); Peter Van Toorn for his poem from *In Guildenstern County* (Delta Canada Press); Miriam Waddington for 'Green World Two'.

Acknowledgements for the Fourth Revision

PERMISSION to use copyright material for this new revision is gratefully acknowledged to the following:

House of Anansi Ltd, Toronto, for 'Nos. 2 & 6' from *Civil Elegies and Other Poems* by Dennis Lee.

Clarke Irwin (1983) Inc., Toronto, for 'A Tiger in the Dublin Zoo' and 'Plot for a science fiction novel' from *Between tears and laughter* by Alden Nowlan.

Dodd, Mead & Company Inc., New York, for 'The Shooting of Dan McGrew' from *The Collected Poems of Robert Service.*

Feinman & Krasilovsky, New York, for 'The Shooting of Dan McGrew' from *The Collected Poems of Robert Service.*

General Publishing Co. Ltd, Don Mills, Ont., for 'Against Description' from *West Window* by George Bowering; 'Tremor' and 'There Is No Place' from *A Throw of Particles* by D. G. Jones; 'The Madwomen of the Plaza de Mayo' and 'The Moon in All Her Phases' from *Dreaming Backwards* by Eli Mandel.

Macmillan of Canada, A Division of Gage Publishing Ltd, for 'Nostalgie de Bonheur' from *Anniversaries* and selections from 'Landslides' from *The Prinzhorn Collection* by Don Coles; 'Silverthorn Bush' from *Silverthorn Bush & Other Poems* by Robert Finch; 'Inside the Great Pyramid' from *Magic Animals: Selected Poems Old and New* by Gwendolyn MacEwen.

McClelland & Stewart Ltd, Toronto, for 'Prairie' and 'Railroad Switching Yard' from *The Presence of Fire* by George Amabile; 'The Bear on the Delhi Road' and 'A Walk in Kyoto' from *Ghost in the Wheels: Selected Poems* by Earle Birney; 'Xenophanes', 'Essay on Adam' and 'Poem about Crystal' from *The Beauty of the Weapons* by Robert Bringhurst; 'Avoiding Greece' and 'Earthquake' from *The Solitary City* by R. A. D. Ford; 'In the Yukon', 'Of Green Steps and Laundry', 'Hyacinths with Brevity', 'A Pile of Grave-Slates', 'Hearing the Woodthrush in the Evening' and 'The Philosophy of the Parthenon' from *The Moment is All: Selected Poems 1944–1983* by Ralph Gustafson; 'Early Morning Sounds' from *A Wild Peculiar Joy: Selected Poems 1945–82* by Irving Layton; 'You Can Climb Down Now' from *The Gods* by Dennis Lee; 'The Double-Headed Snake' from *The Fat Man: Selected Poems 1962–1972* by John Newlove; 'Lament for the Dorsets', 'The Country North of Belleville' and 'Necropsy of Love' from *Al Purdy: Selected Poems*; 'Wart Hog' from *Timelight* by Robin Skelton; 'The Lonely Land' from *The Classic Shade* by A. J. M. Smith; 'Alias Rock Dove, Alias Holy Ghost' and 'Pool' from *Birding, or Desire* by Don McKay.

McGraw-Hill Ryerson Ltd, Toronto, for 'Eve', 'The Uninvited', 'Rowan Red Rowan' and 'Waking in the Dark' from *Collected Poems: The Two Seasons* by Dorothy Livesay; 'The Shooting of Dan McGrew' from *The Collected Poems of Robert Service.*

Mosaic Press/Valley Editions, Oakville, Ont., for 'Tall Tales' from *The T. E. Lawrence Poems* by Gwendolyn MacEwen; 'Before Passover' and 'Birthday' from *The Impossible Promised Land* by Seymour Mayne; and 'The Cable' from *Stones in Water* by David Solway.

Oberon Press, Ottawa, for 'Where I Come From' and 'There Is Time' from *Sometimes I Think of Moving* by Elizabeth Brewster; 'Lot', 'The Jockeys' and 'The Death of Harlequin' from *The Sign of the Gunman* by David Helwig; 'Reminder' from *The Island Man* by George McWhirter; 'Eight Pears' and 'On the Edge' from *Extra Innings* by Raymond Souster; and 'Politics' from *The Elements* by Tom Marshall.

Oxford University Press, Toronto, for 'Variations on the Word Sleep' from *True Stories* by Margaret Atwood; 'Camping' from *Driving Home* by Miriam Waddington; 'The Day-Labourer' from *The Boatman* by Jay Macpherson; 'One Last Word' from *Selected Poems* by John Glassco.

Talon Books, Vancouver, for 'The Days of the Unicorns' and 'Ezra Pound' from *The Vision Tree: Selected Poems* by Phyllis Webb.

Grateful acknowledgement is made to the following authors: Milton Acorn for 'Knowing I live in a Dark Age' from *Jawbreakers*, 'Old Property' and 'Whale Poem' from *The Island Means Minago* (New Canada Press, Toronto); Margaret Avison for 'Hid Life' from *Sunblue* (Lancelot Press, Hantsport, N.S.); Doug Beardsley for his poems; bill bissett for his poems from *plutonium missing* (blewointment press, Vancouver); George Bowering for 'In the Elevator' from *The Concrete Island* (Vehicule Press, Montreal); R. G. Everson for his poems; Marya Fiamengo for 'For Osip Mandelstam' and 'The High Cost of Eternity'; Lionel Kearns for 'Captivity' and 'International Incident' from *Ignoring the Bomb* (Oolichan Books, Lantzville, B.C.); Robert Kroetsch for 'There is a World' and 'Anthem' from *Seed Catalogue* (Turnstone Press, Winnipeg, Man.); Patrick Lane for 'The Carpenter' from *Poems New & Selected* (Oxford University Press, Toronto); Charles Lillard for his poems from *Drunk on Wood and Other Poems* and *Voice My Shaman* (Sono Nis Press, Victoria, B.C.); Don McKay for his poems; Alden Nowlan estate for 'The Bull Moose' from *Playing the Jesus Game* (New Books, Trumansburg, N.Y.); Michael Ondaatje for 'Country Night' from *There's a Trick with a Knife I'm Learning to Do* (McClelland & Stewart, Toronto); Al Purdy for 'The Blue City'; Joe Rosenblatt for 'Fish' from *Top Soil* (Press Porcepic, Erin, Ont.); David Solway for 'The Lame Diver' from *Selected Poems* (Vehicule Press, Montreal, Que.).

Doug Beardsley has been kind enough to choose the selections from my work. Diligent inquiry has been made to establish the owners of copyright material; if anyone has been overlooked, the editor makes sincere apologies.

R. G.

The Pelican Anthology of Canadian Poetry

London, England
1942

Preface

SOME readers will find many omissions in this anthology. Others, I trust, will welcome its emphasis on certain Canadian poetry not heretofore adequately represented. Most non-Canadians will be surprised to learn that Canadian poetry exists at all. It is my hope that this anthology will persuade them to an eager acknowledgement.

In my task as compiler, I have had to forgo, obviously, much good poetry; have had honestly to reject material that had become falsely established. The yardstick for my task was plain and unvarnished. I have measured and judged each poem not by historical significance nor by 'Canadianism', but in terms of vitality: is it *alive* or *dead*? If it deepened experience, caught the heart and mind with beauty they 'would not willingly let die' – and was technically exciting – in it went. I have tried to have nothing to do with static conventionality, apings and 'poetics', *cliché* and acrobatics.

Canadian literature is relatively young: a natural but indulgent self-consciousness has characterized many of its poets and critics. It was remembered that the nation's poetry *is* Canada; it was forgotten that 'Canadianism' is not necessarily a poem. But that is past. A Canadian poet can no longer consider that his poem derives importance solely because it is *written*; his increasing individuality has outgrown a former imitativeness of the pre-1914 English poetic convention; he has a critical familiarity with poetic advances in the United States and England; a kinetic sensitivity to his social environment – these factors have produced a Canadian poetry which is urgent, which can exist as poetry while remaining (not only geographically) distinguishable as Canadian.

I am hoping, above all, that the poems herein will become synonymous with *pleasure* – startle with a fine excess of beauty; that they will compel the reader to search out the books from which these examples have been selected. It needs to be said again: poetry is neither stuffily solemn, scholastic, nor an esoteric controversy for 'poets' to segregate themselves over. It is the stuff of life.

RALPH GUSTAFSON

January 1941

From the Introduction to the 1957 Revision

CANADIAN poetry has had self-respect and integrity from the first. One assumes that any poetry has. But the assertion is well made in connection with Canadian poetry. There is a prevailing ignorance that supposes the opposite. The prejudice exists largely in the opinion that Canadian poetry is a feeble and pale reflection of the British poetic scene, that it is, in its later manifestation, obedient to American poetic activity and conveniently supplanted by it. The present anthology offers a hundred years of Canadian poetry. It is a poetry of distinction.

The poet cannot be asked to find his national identity before the factors that present it to him exist. Canadian poets identifiable as such, have had to wait for Canada. Canadian poetry came to maturity slowly and with difficulty. Slowly, since the making of a Canadian existence was late and vast; with difficulty, since the population which could support a culture was meagre and because the urgent preoccupation with commerce and industry vitiated its values. The stifling of the creative arts stifled self-recognition. Canadian poetry existed by virtue of its own integrity.

Meanwhile, in the sense of the handing down of an ethos, two traditions, the British and the French, were viable. English-Canadian writers wrote naturally in the belief that they were a part of the heritage that includes the author of *Beowulf* and Chaucer. They still do. Tradition in the sense of formal ceremonies, cricket instead of lacrosse, Canadians began diverging from long ago.

The confusion that to recognize a tradition as natural is an imitation, has led a number of critics into a great deal of waste motion. They are afraid that this is colonial-mindedness, Canadian poetry the likeness of the poor British relation that rather disgracefully but happily left for the colonies. There is much poetry in Canada that fits the picture. It is all bad poetry. Why deal with it? The assumption by good Canadian poets that the British spiritual heritage was natural to them is another matter. It upsets high-strung patriotic critics. Early Canadian poets, born abroad, were nostalgic. Canada was a wild and big place. There is a great deal in their poems of Do the bourns of the glens still waggle. They wanted to know. But they also looked around them. None of them in this book is colonial-minded. The earlier poets were sensitive that they were not a nation of achieved greatness, they therefore sometimes exhort in a parochial and non-poetic manner. This is left-hand evidence they are not colonial-minded. They liked what they saw. They accepted what was not an affectation. The British tradition of justice is satisfactory to Canadians. So is Wordsworth's way of looking at a daffodil – the daffodil grows in Canada. Canada did not hunt nightingales. The tomato is not the tomayto. In the United States, that is very British. The Canadians think nothing of it and eat it, very often, with sugar, which is very unBritish.

The fact that nineteenth-century Canadian poets wrote in the manner of the nineteenth century has bothered the critics. They let the imitators upset them. Valid Canadian poets, immigrant or native born, started where they had to: with the traditions of imaginative attack and the conventions of technique of their immediate predecessors or contemporaries elsewhere. There is in these valid poets a great deal that is imitative, that is not even emulative. Keats, Tennyson, Arnold, and Emerson were overwhelming. But they had tough personalities, these early Canadian poets, and they looked where they wanted to. In scathing verse Isabella Valancy Crawford looked into General Wolseley's war on the Zulus under Cetewayo; Isabella Valancy Crawford was a young woman living in obscurity in Toronto. She also almost made a myth out of the forests and weather of wild Ontario. She wrote a neo-Classic narrative poem. Charles G. D. Roberts wrote another. It was being done. Their samples can compare with any. Lampman wrote sonnets like any of his contemporaries, they are as good and better; untransplantable sonnets that cannot be mistaken as other than Canadian. Neither can Roberts's.

Canadian poetry divides roughly into three main periods; each has the same integrity, the same skilful moderation that is aware of the continuity of its heritage, a recalcitrance of personality; the last period, the cumulative identity that is Canadian.

The earliest verses written in Canada are lively and loyal, but none is to be found in this book. There are some nice turns of wit and satire, there are some vivid lines on early Canadian settler life, but the poetry is unexceptional. The substantial beginning was made by the Three Charleses – Heavysege, Sangster, and Mair. Heavysege is a considerable poet. His major work is a closet drama, *Saul*. The hero struggles against his destiny without having made it, the drama is without the conditions for tragedy. Much of the writing is transcription. But when

Heavysege gets away from his Biblical texts, the drama takes on a power that is impressive.

Charles Sangster states quite simply, 'I love my art'. The strength, in a few poems, is felt. Charles Mair had a burning love of Canada, and when he wrote of the details of homes and nature around him, achieved a fine effect.

With the Group of the Sixties – poets born near the Confederation of 1867 who came to their maturity in the 1890s: Roberts, Lampman, Carman, Duncan Campbell Scott – Canada gained poets who were national. A Canadian literature was being created. Each of this group wrote fluently and well, often exceedingly well. There was technical excellence, a less innocent national awareness, definition of nature and locality, a compassion and virility, and a united dedication to the art of poetry. Canada could not be, after them, careless of her culture.

There is much inferior work in the Group of the Sixties, they were prolific poets. Roberts overstrains his Emersonian striving toward a cosmic consciousness; Lampman is a poet of one theme; Carman, largely, is at his worst in the poems which present themselves as his best, when he is capturing the 'oversoul' and is down the lanes as a fine vagabond; Duncan Campbell Scott wrote perhaps too occasionally. Each can be run back obviously to Keats, Shelley, Tennyson, Arnold, Emerson.

But the scholarly pursuit of derivation is a game for 'the blind book-worm', as Lampman has him. 'The feeling of delight is the thing, not its cause', says Duncan Campbell Scott. And if the adverse criticism is placed here, it is to safeguard the statement that these poets are each, in his scope, as distinguished poets as North America has produced. In his earlier poetry – where Roberts is rooted to his Tantramar – and in certain of his later poems wherein the New Brunswick scene is revisited, Roberts is at his most impressive; in his sensitive evocation of the rural scene, his depth of imagination, his fine ear, and humble nobility of spirit. Lampman is supreme in his great subject, the land-scape – the landscape of Ontario – the natural beauty of the world and the sorrow and loneliness of man who inhabits it. He is a master of the sonnet. In Carman's best is a clear, beautiful music, an honesty that is the daring of innocence, and over all, a joyousness of spirit and a gentleness of soul that are heedlessly winning – an imagination which Lampman found 'that of our own northern land'. The poetry of Duncan Campbell Scott is of a man who loved life wholly, affectionately, and at all times; where the word in Lampman is dream, the word in Duncan Campbell Scott is memory; he is a technician of refinement. In 'The Piper of Arll' he has written one of the few successful poems of poetry as music – a ballad of the fatal possession by the world of the beauty which longs to be one with it.

They were long-lived poets. Lampman apart, all but the youngest of today's poets could have known them. They were in the romantic tradition. One or two good poets, like Marjorie Pickthall, lingered in a sort of purple afterglow; but Romanticism was done. The majority belonging to the span of years before the century got well started, trying to write out the romantic tradition, were, or are, too late.

Striding the breach of accomplishment to new accomplishment is a redoubtable poet, E. J. Pratt. A master narrator, a technician of splendour and man of compassion and ironic depth, Pratt is one of the outstanding figures of Canadian writing. The pace, scope, dauntlessness, and comedy – Canada is everywhere in him. Suddenly, someone was writing:

> A bull moose that had died from gas
> While eating toadstools near Ungava.

The thrust of personality onto the poetic scene was grand. The sweep and buckle of obstructive satire entered Canadian verse; a sense of comedy burbled the Pierian springs; machines were admitted; a narrative irony was existent. E. J. Pratt is a poet of heroic proportions, not an epic poet, but epic in scope; not a tragic poet, but a poet with a profound sense of tragedy. Canada was being defined. In 1928, W. W. E. Ross's 'northern' poems were written, setting forth precisely, with wonder and freshness, and in verse that broke away from the old conventions, the changing qualities of Canada's natural scene. Raymond Knister was writing his poems of rural Ontario.

The publication in 1936 of a slim anthology called *New Provinces*, presenting the work of Finch, Kennedy, Klein, Pratt, F. R. Scott, and A. J. M. Smith, dispelled any illusion that the methods of thought and technique that had prevailed, stretching back from the Georgians to the nineteenth-century romanticism, were adequate to express the contemporary scene; trips to the Canadian fields and streams in a wondrous frame of mind would no longer do. The literary techniques, the advances of Yeats and Eliot, were assimilated by the *New Provinces* poets; wit came in, science, satire, and precision. An immediate social context was made essential.

In the 1940s, there was an invigoration. Protest – social, environmental, personal, economic – was strenuously voiced. The First World War had shaken individual faiths and beliefs. The Second World War smashed values wholesale. Personality, for its survival, was thrown on toughness of character. Canadian poets showed it. The Canadian poets of the forties demanded dignity, personal and social, buttressed it, defended it, and published it. With angry conviction, they stuck to values, like love, uncommercialized Christmas, unconformity, time not speed; they resented the stapled forms of Life, Peek, and Digest. Layton identified himself with the truth that the natural man is a creation of nobility, Dudek and Souster were a proof that spiritual toughness is compassion. Earle Birney, Klein, F. R. Scott, A. J. M. Smith, wrote with continuing force of the times and the desperate need of the times. They are accomplished technically. Their phrasing is Canadian. It is becoming increasingly apparent that Canada has a poetry that is distinctly her own.

What is Canadian? The specifics of contemporary Canadian poetry are these:

> The sea, primal, challenging, present.
> Diving, literal diving, diving back to; an astounding
> engagement with water dived into.
> Green: as an amazing engagement: green blood, green air, green
> out of the white of winter.
> Hills, despite the prairies, granite and the antagonist,
> the Laurentian Shield.
> A hatred of cruelty, of cruelty to cruelty.
> Women make men.
> The eye: symbol and *active* agent.
> Concern with fish symbolic; not religion.
> War is not a natural condition
> A laughter toward tourists.
> Little longing for diviner regions.
> (Only one Mountie – in a satire; one snowshoe.)

These are the main objective correlatives and attitudes. They add up, not without comedy, into the word, north.

This method of thought, pattern of feeling, distinguishes the verbal texture of the modern Canadian poem. The 'phrasing', the 'fingering' – which determines the phrasing, as the pianist knows – is different; the Canadian 'phrasing' is not the American, it is certainly not the English. F. R. Scott's 'Old Song' gives the Canadian 'fingering' plain;

so do W. W. E. Ross's 'The Walk' and 'The Fish'. So does A. J. M. Smith's 'The Lonely Land'. The difference in 'musculature' – to shift the terms from music – is found everywhere in Pratt; is unmistakable in Earle Birney's 'Bushed'.

There is the difference in 'intimacy' with nature. There are no Aphrodites in Canadian poetry – the seafoam is too cold. The Furies have to be imported. The Laurentian Shield is the intruder. There are no places for yearlong thought in a green shade.

We are hitched to the seasons – four sharp ones with no south to melt into. After ice-lockings, we dive into spring. Conditions are good for spare lyricism, metaphysical wit; for an essential stability; for the green from the white.

This book presents itself as a survey, from the first to the latest, of English-Canadian poetry. This does not mean all excellent poetry is represented, nor that the poet included has not written other poems of equal quality. I should like to have given more space to the poets (or some of them); but there are mechanical limits. I regret cutting lines out of dramas and narratives. The book differs from my previous Penguin Anthology, the earlier poets more solidly represented, the periods better balanced. I have still, however, emphasized contemporary poetry. It is where we live.

RALPH GUSTAFSON

New York, 1957

From the Foreword to the Revised 1966 Edition

This revised edition, coinciding with Canada's own Centennial, presents a survey of the work done in English by Canadian poets during the past one hundred years. Twenty-five years ago when the *Pelican Anthology of Canadian Poetry* introduced and published abroad the work of English-Canadian poets, the survey was made with comparative ease. There was then nothing like the present national vitality in manuscripts, readings, subsidies, prizes, broadsheets, pamphlets, private presses, periodicals, and books of poetry from the commercial houses. Centres of activity were few and localized. Isolation was the problem: pretty much as it was in Lampman's day. The general cultural climate of Canada was one of provincialism, complacency, or indifference. During the decade following World War II, those negative forces were well in retreat. The first revision of this book in 1957 was able to take advantage of a true perspective of the past, a present of rich provision, and assume a confidence in the future which one or two critics, deploying themselves from abroad, felt bound to temper. The confidence has been proved anything but misplaced. The last ten years have produced a poetry that makes historical all questioning of Canada's poetic calibre.

Editors in England and the United States of those comprehensive anthologies of 'English' poetry still ignore the work of Canadian poets Readers should not be misled or let themselves be unconcerned. The compulsion of a figure in Canada comparable to T. S. Eliot or Ezra Pound is lacking. But the Canadian occupation is distinguished and distinguishable. I have further thoughts on what is 'Canadian'; but the premises already set forth need not be altered. The distinctive quality which I defined (not without comedy) is 'northness' (the music of Sibelius has 'northness'). And I oppose the boredom of those critics who are convinced that it does not matter who we are.

Despair is universal over the question of who everyone is. It is necessary to know. We have got ourselves into a position where perhaps this is possible. Disillusion is irreducible; the inherited past is totally questioned. Now something is happening. So radically have protests been lodged that the negations are proving no longer sufficient. We are in the midst, or at the beginning of the re-creation. The dialogue of the new Canadian poets is of the greatest interest. The burden is testamentary. It is Jonah getting himself out of the whale, caught between allegiance to a secure cynicism and declarations of his own future. The determination is not to be negated. By those who want disillusioned affirmation, these fresh sensibilities are not to be ignored.

Technically, the swing is from the Yeats/Eliot axis to the Pound/Williams axis. Yeats had the leisure to prophesy and warn of the Second Coming with traditional formality. These poets have not. They are in the midst of the advent of the Pitiless Beast. Immediacy and objectism are the demands; freedom from the traditional prosodic formalities. Hence, Ezra Pound and his renovations: the shift in poetic processes from 'formal' to 'open' composition. The correct objective is the achievement of greater and swifter immediacy in presenting experience; of minimal interference with the instant of cognition. The appeal is to music, 'to compose in sequence of the musical phrase, not in sequence of a metronome', as Ezra Pound put it; to overcome the displacement of tempos by metres; to overcome statics. It is to strive toward the condition of music. We return to the aesthetic of Pater, at least in this respect.

Poetry, however, is not music. Two mistakes are made. First, the error of thinking that notation is music; secondly, the error of thinking that language can communicate as music communicates. It can't. Poetry uses language. However much we strain to prevent it, poetry to be itself carries a burden of logical meaning. Music uses aural structures and is thereby dramatic. This language cannot do. Without its integument of syntax and grammatical structure, the poem is undramatic. Without the drama of syntax there is no tension. Poetry must resolve more than sound and rhythm; it must also resolve its linguistic meaning. I do not find this sad. I find this inevitable. The poet has the greater challenge.

This misadventure with music has led to the broken line, the jettisoning of metre, the placement of spaces and rests and pauses on the printed page which have so bemused and bewildered the conventional reader. The advantages gained have been several: natural breathing, 'the pressures of the breath', the physiology of cadence, modulations and juxtapositions. Mostly, these 'liberated' poems are unholy messes – the result of not perceiving the difference between music and language, the typewriter and rhythm, the lungs and the intellect:

D. H. Lawrence's 'swoonings' and Eliot's *Quartets* (I am not being religious).

Poetry is at one with music in structuring beautiful sound, and this sound is also the meaning. The errors are in mistaking notation for music and in mistaking the conditions of music for those of language.

My criteria in judging such adventure (vitality) consist of three negatives. I consider dead (though it may look alive typographically) the poem (1) in which the liberation (disenfranchising of syntax, referants, metre, punctuation, or whatever convention) defeats communication, or so delays it that the poem is injured, or so assumes an arrogance that the reader is left to write the poem: when the theoretical poetry is so inaccessible that Frost's 'immortal wound' has to be self-inflicted; (2) in which the structure or the lack of structure of the line goes against natural phrasing, the instinctive physiological *and* (*nota bene*) intellectual pacing; (3) in which the manipulation is not accumulation and is not worth the poetry gained.

It is toil, this poetry. And, says Pound: 'Mais d'abord il faut être un poète'.

Bishop's University, 1966 RALPH GUSTAFSON

Preface to the Fourth Revision

WITHIN the limits of space and the criterion set, this revision has been able to present the work of the established contemporary names in English-Canadian poetry in its advances and to include twelve poets new to the pages of this book. The vitality of Canadian poetry is strong.

The standard of judgement used for the selection is set forth in the previous forewords. It has determined the exclusion made in the course of reading the almost jostling number of books of poetry being published in Canada. One increasing danger became apparent. It involves the interplay between the poet and the public, the craft and its value to the social context in which it exists. There is a danger in the practice of contemporary poetry.

Poetry is an art. There is no use thinking of it otherwise. A poem is a highly crafted verbal communication that prevents confusion and transmits delight. Its ordering makes life more sensible. Hence the delight.

The intelligent and delighting structure is achieved by a balance and tension of words brought to a superior movement in time. To use the words of the craft, this cannot be done without the transaction between metre and rhythm (the bar-line and slur in music), a controlled pace that is itself the pace and depth of the emotion felt. A statement cannot do this, reason cannot do it, technical disdain cannot do it, nor innocence, arrogance and the subconscious. The practised imagination alone can do it. But it must be through the captured freedom of rhythm against denial, the obstacle overcome that creates liberation. Without this opposition there is neither tension nor resolution; without this presentation of emotion there is no poetic power. Without this kind of delight there is no poem.

The procedure is simple.

There is a prevalent danger. The claim is made that the value of a poem is in the degree of the elimination of the art. The atavistic claim produces self-reverence; how the poet creates is arrogantly thought to be of more value than what it achieves; broken prose is thought to be rhythm; syntactical incoherence is declared to be communication.

The social effect of poetry is defeated.

That must not happen.

R. G.

North Hatley, 1983

OLIVER GOLDSMITH

1794–1861

From *The Rising Village*

What noble courage must their hearts have fired,
How great the ardour which their souls inspired,
Who, leaving far behind their native plain,
Have sought a home beyond the western main;
And braved the terrors of the stormy seas,
In search of wealth, of freedom, and of ease!
Oh! none can tell but they who sadly share
The bosom's anguish, and its wild despair,
What dire distress awaits the hardy bands
That venture first on bleak and desert lands;
How great the pain, the danger, and the toil
Which mark the first rude culture of the soil.
When, looking round, the lonely settler sees
His home amid a wilderness of trees:
How sinks his heart in those deep solitudes,
When not a voice upon his ear intrudes;
Where solemn silence all the waste pervades,
Heightening the horror of its gloomy shades;
Save where the sturdy woodman's strokes resound,
That strew the fallen forest on the ground.
See! from their heights the lofty pines descend,
And crackling, down their pond'rous lengths extend.
Soon from their boughs the curling flames arise,
Mount into air, and redden all the skies;
And where the forest once its foliage spread,
The golden corn triumphant waves its head . . .

Happy Acadia! though around thy shore
Is heard the stormy wind's terrific roar;
Though round thee Winter binds his icy chain,
And his rude tempests sweep along thy plain,
Still Summer comes, and decorates thy land
With fruits and flowers from her luxuriant hand;
Still Autumn's gifts repay the labourer's toil

With richest products from thy fertile soil;
With bounteous store his varied wants supply,
And scarce the plants of other suns deny,
How pleasing, and how glowing with delight
Are now thy budding hopes! How sweetly bright
They rise to view! How full of joy appear
The expectations of each future year!
Not fifty Summers yet have blessed thy clime,
How short a period in the page of time!
Since savage tribes, with terror in their train,
Rushed o'er thy fields, and ravaged all thy plain,
But some few years have rolled in haste away
Since, through thy vales, the fearless beast of prey,
With dismal yell and loud appalling cry,
Proclaimed his midnight reign of terror nigh.
And now how changed the scene! the first afar,
Have fled to wilds beneath the northern star;
The last has learned to shun man's dreaded eye,
And, in his turn, to distant regions fly.
While the poor peasant, whose laborious care
Scarce from the soil could wring his scanty fare;
Now in the peaceful arts of culture skilled,
Sees his wide barn with ample treasures filled;
Now finds his dwelling, as the year goes round,
Beyond his hopes, with joy and plenty crowned . . .

Dear lovely spot! Oh may such charms as these,
Sweet tranquil charms, that cannot fail to please,
Forever reign around thee, and impart
Joy, peace, and comfort to each native heart.

CHARLES HEAVYSEGE

1816–76

From *Saul*

(Malzah, *the Evil Spirit from the Lord*)

Ah, weary! I am called the laughing devil.
Yet I walk up and down existence weeping . . .
How like is man unto the fallen angels!
How many in my mood now walk this world!
Some sullen at their fellows, some at fate –
From which there is no more escaping than
There is from our free wills; and some are sad
With envy at another's good, and some
With unfulfilled ambition; some with hate
Are sad, and some with love unlucky; some
With fear of missing heaven, some with dread
Of falling into hell; and many more
With curious worldly cares:- and here come Saul
And Jonathan, and both of them dejected.
We were a mournful trio, should I join them:
Grave as three owls, as sober as three storks,
More gloomy than a trinity of ravens.
In spirit, truly pitiful they show;
Portentous in appearance as yon heavens;
Or as two doctors, weighing if their patient
Shall die or live. I will approach, and listen . . .

(*The Hebrew Camp*. Saul muses.)

O life, how delicate a thing thou art,
Crushed with the feathery edge of a thin blade!
Frail! – why wert thou not made inviolable?
Why art thou irrecoverable as frail?
Thou, noblest guest, art all as much exposed
To foul ejectment from the flesh as is
The spider from its web by maiden's broom.
Yea, with a little wielded iron, any
Can drive thee forth from thy recesses' walls,

Which thou wilt not repair; for thou, weak fool,
At voice of death, from thine old banquet-room
Start'st like a haughty noble that, in huff,
Leaves his convives, and will return no more.
Why should I cherish thee, why feed thee now!
Yet I, a breathing corse, must mumble – I,
A shadow, raise my sunken, phantom maw
With the refection of this solid world . . .
All have gone from me now except despair;
And my last, lingering relics of affection –

(*After weeping awhile in silence*)

Now let me scorn all further tenderness;
And keep my heart as obdurate as the hills,
That have endured the assault of every tempest
Poured on them from the founding of the world.

(*A trumpet sounds*)

Now let me die, for I indeed was slain
With my three sons.

From *Count Filippo*

(*Of Hylas who has fallen head over heels in love with Volina*)

GALLANTIO: Now let the drums roll muffled; let the bells'
Shrill tongues toll mournfully for Hylas slain!
But though all nature should put mourning on,
Though drums be garnished with funereal crape,
My brows shall wear no less their native rose;
Though rusty drops should from the bells descend,
Dappling the upturned throats of thirsty ringers,
Adown mine own no less red wine shall flow!
We'll pledge the genius of ill luck – why not?
And draw bright laughter out of dull defeat.
PAPHIANA: Thou hast a nobler spirit than the prince. –
But is it true he plays the moribond?
GALLANTIO: Dead, dead! shot, shot to death, Paph, shot.

Yes, fairly shot, all foully shot, hath been
This representative of thirty dukes;
Each a contemner both of dart and gun.
Dead, dead is Hylas; shot, young Hylas, shot;
Banished into the air, Paph; blown point-blank
Into the world-wide welkin, shattered, shivered.
All shattered, shivered, shot; oh; shooting shame!
Shot with the bombshell of Volina's eyelid.
PAPHIANA: See here the power of woman when she wills.
GALLANTIO: True, you are powerful, and can sting like nettles,
When you are plucked by over-fearful fingers.
Volina hath her would-be stinger stung;
Teased him, as a tormenting wasp or bee
Might, in the flowery meadow, tease the steer;
Bled him to death, as butcher might a calf, –
Full many a calf hath less deserved the butcher,
Full many a butcher better quitted Cupid;
Who's shot my blue-eyed booby out of ambush;
Couching, like painted Indian 'midst the reeds,
In covert of Volina's dark eyelashes.
Now let him puff with pride of sovereign blood.
Oh, sovereign blood! oh, blood of thirty sovereigns!
Who now would give a penny for a pint
Of sovereign blood? Paph, not a pint of blood
Is in his carcass left, with love-shot riddled.
PAPHIANA: The hunter's self hath e'en been hunted down, –
The deer he stalked hath given him a gore.
GALLANTIO: Most grieviously hath gored him; – but I've lost
Now faith in elegants; believe what's told
Of stalwart Samson by Delilah bound;
Of Hercules to spinning set with maids;
Of Jacob, too, who twice seven years to Laban
Did bind himself apprentice for his wives.
These bonds are good, since Hylas hath endorsed them.
PAPHIANA: These all are holy writ. But something, perhaps,
Has been forgotten in the prince's mould;
As in his ducking was Achilles' heel.
GALLANTIO: He's no Achilles, though she is a Helen, –
No Caesar he, though she as Cleopatra;
Volina lonely lingering in her bower,

Rose-pillowed, match of Egypt's magic queen. –
But as Marc Antony did lose the world
To win grand Cleopatra, so hath Hylas
Now lost his heart but hath not won Volina.

Song from *Count Filippo*

Who is lord of lordly fate, –
Lady of her lot's estate?
He who rules himself is he,
She who tempts not fate is she.

Who in peril stands of pain?
Who is sure to suffer stain?
He who climbs a thorny tree,
Gathers juicy berries she.

'*The stars are glittering in the frosty sky*'

The stars are glittering in the frosty sky,
Frequent as pebbles on a broad sea-coast;
And o'er the vault the cloud-like galaxy
Has marshalled its innumerable host.
Alive all heaven seems! with wondrous glow
Tenfold refulgent every star appears,
As if some wide, celestial gale did blow,
And thrice illume the ever-kindled spheres.
Orbs, with glad orbs rejoicing, burning, beam,
Ray-crowned, with lambent lustre in their zones,
Till o'er the blue, bespangled spaces seem
Angels and great archangels on their thrones;
A host divine, whose eyes are sparkling gems,
And forms more bright than diamond diadems.

ALEXANDER McLACHLAN

1818–96

'O! come to the greenwood shade'

O! come to the greenwood shade,
  Away from the city's din,
From the heartless strife of trade,
  And the fumes of beer and gin;
Where commerce spreads her fleets,
  Where bloated luxury lies,
And Want as she prowls the streets,
  Looks on with her wolfish eyes.

From the city with its sin,
  And its many coloured code,
Its palaces raised to gin,
  And its temples reared to God;
Its cellars dark and dank,
  Where never a sunbeam falls,
Amid faces lean and lank,
  As the hungry-looking walls.

Its festering pits of woe,
  Its teeming earthly hells,
Whose surges ever flow,
  In sound of the Sabbath bells!
O God! I would rather be
  An Indian in the wood,
And range through the forest free,
  In search of my daily food.

O! rather would I pursue,
  The wolf and the grizzly bear,
Than toil for the thankless few,
  In those seething pits of care;
Here winter's breath is rude,
  And his fingers cold and wan;

But what is his wildest mood,
  To the tyranny of man?

To the trackless forest wild,
  To the loneliest abode;
O! the heart is reconciled,
  That has felt oppression's load!
The desert place is bright,
  The wilderness is fair,
If hope but shed her light, –
  If freedom be but there.

CHARLES SANGSTER

1822–93

From *The St Lawrence and the Saguenay*

On, through the lovely Archipelago,
Glides the swift bark. Soft summer matins ring
From every isle. The wild fowl come and go,
Regardless of our presence On the wing,
And perched upon the boughs, the gay birds sing
Their loves: This is their summer paradise;
From morn till night their joyous caroling
Delights the ear, and through the lucent skies
Ascends the choral hymn in softest symphonies.

The Spring is gone – light, genial-hearted Spring!
Whose breath gives odor to the violet,
Crimsons the wild rose, tints the blackbird's wing,
Unfolds the buttercup. Spring that has set
To music the laughter of the rivulet,
Sent warm pulsations through the hearts of hills,
Reclothed the forests, made the valleys wet
With pearly dew, and waked the grave old mills
From their calm sleep, by the loud rippling of the rills.

Long years ago the early Voyageurs
Gladdened these wilds with some romantic air;
The moonlight, dancing on their dripping oars,
Showed the slow batteaux passing by with care,
Impelled by rustic crews, as debonnair
As ever struck pale Sorrow dumb with Song:
Many a drooping spirit longed to share
Their pleasant melodies, that swept among
The echo-haunted woods, in accents clear and strong . . .

And now 'tis Night. A myriad stars have come
To cheer the earth, and sentinel the skies,
The full-orbed moon irradiates the gloom,
And fills the air with light. Each Islet lies
Immersed in shadow, soft as thy dark eyes;

Swift through the sinuous path our vessel glides,
Now hidden by the massive promontories,
Anon the bubbling silver from its sides
Spurning, like a wild bird, whose home is on the tides . . .

The distant knolls are soft as midnight clouds
Filled with bright memories of departed day.
Like purple glories rolling up the woods,
This rugged wilderness which we survey
Extends in wild, magnificent array,
To regions rarely trod by mortal feet.
Ev'n here, love, though we would, we cannot stay;
We cannot loiter near this calm retreat;
The Morn approaches, and his fiery steeds are fleet.

From *Sonnets*

Written in the Orillia Woods, August 1859

Blest Spirit of Calm that dwellest in these woods!
Thou art a part of that serene repose
That ofttimes lingers in the solitudes
Of my lone heart, when the tumultuous throes
Of some vast Grief have borne me to the earth.
For I have fought with Sorrow face to face;
Have tasted of the cup that brings to some
A frantic madness and delirious mirth,
But prayed and trusted for the light to come,
To break the gloom and darkness of the place.
Through the dim aisles the sunlight penetrates,
And nature's self rejoices; heaven's light
Comes down into my heart, and in its might
My soul stands up and knocks at God's own temple-gates.

CHARLES MAIR

1838–1927

Winter

When gadding snow makes hill-sides white,
  And icicles form more and more;
When niggard Frost stands all the night,
  And taps at snoring Gaffer's door;
When watch-dogs bay the vagrant wind,
  And shiv'ring kine herd close in shed;
When kitchens chill, and maids unkind,
  Send rustic suitors home to bed –
    Then do I say the winter cold,
    It seems to me, is much too bold.

When winking sparks run up the stalk,
  And faggots blaze within the grate,
And, by the ingle-cheek, I talk
  With shadows from the realm of fate;
When authors old, yet ever young,
  Look down upon me from the walls,
And songs by spirit-lips are sung
  To pleasant tunes and madrigals, –
    Then do I say the winter cold
    Brings back to me the joys of old.

When morn is bleak, and sunshine cool,
  And trav'llers' beards with rime are grey;
When frost-nipt urchins weep in school,
  And sleighs creak o'er the drifted way;
When smoke goes quick from chimney-top,
  And mist flies through the open hatch;
When snow-flecks to the window hop,
  And children's tongues cling to the latch, –
    Then do I sigh for summer wind,
    And wish the winter less unkind.

When merry bells a-jingling go,
  And prancing horses beat the ground;

When youthful hearts are all aglow,
  And youthful gladness rings around;
When gallants praise, and maidens blush
  To hear their charms so loudly told,
Whilst echoing vale and echoing bush
  Halloo their laughter, fold on fold, –
    Then do I think the winter meet,
    For gallants free and maidens sweet.

When great pines crack with mighty sound,
  And ice doth rift with doleful moan;
When luckless wanderers are found
  Quite stiff in wooded valleys lone;
When ragged mothers have no sheet
  To shield their babes from winter's flaw;
When milk is frozen in the teat,
  And beggars shiver in their straw, –
    Then do I hate the winter's cheer,
    And weep for springtime of the year.

When ancient hosts their guests do meet,
  And fetch old jorums from the bin;
When viols loud and dancers' feet
  In lofty halls make mickle din;
When jokes pass round, and nappy ale
  Sends pleasure mounting to the brain;
When hours are filched from night so pale,
  And youngsters sigh and maids are fain, –
    Then do I hail the wintry breeze
    Which brings such ripened joys as these.

But, when the winter chills my friend,
  And steals the heart-fire from his breast;
Or woos the ruffian wind to send
  One pang to rob him of his rest –
All gainless grows the Christmas cheer,
  And gloomy seems the new year's light,
For joy but lives when friends are near,
  And dies when they do quit the sight –
    Then, winter, do I cry, 'thy greed
    Is great, ay, thou art cold indeed!'

From *Tecumseh*

(*A grove in front of General Harrison's House, Vincennes, Indiana Territory*)

TECUMSEH: Once we were strong.
Once all this mighty continent was ours,
And the Great Spirit made it for our use.
He knew no boundaries, so had we peace
In the vast shelter of His handiwork,
And, happy here, we cared not whence we came.
We brought no evils thence – no treasured hate,
No greed of gold, no quarrels over God;
And so our broils, to narrow issues joined,
Were soon composed, and touched the ground of peace.
Our very ailments, rising from the earth,
And not from any foul abuse in us,
Drew back, and let age ripen to death's hand.
Thus flowed our lives until your people came,
Till from the East our matchless misery came!
Since then our tale is crowded with your crimes,
With broken faith, with plunder of reserves –
The sacred remnants of our wide domain –
With tamp'rings, and delirious feasts of fire,
The fruit of your thrice-cursed stills of death,
Which make our good men bad, our bad men worse,
Aye! blind them till they grope in open day,
And stumble into miserable graves.
Oh, it is piteous, for none will hear!
There is no hand to help, no heart to feel,
No tongue to plead for us in all your land.
But every hand aims death, and every heart,
Ulcered with hate, resents our presence here;
And every tongue cries for our children's land
To expiate their crime of being born.
Oh, we have ever yielded in the past,
But we shall yield no more! Those plains are ours!
Those forests are our birth-right and our home!
Let not the Long-Knife build one cabin there –
Or fire from it will spread to every roof,
To compass you, and light your souls to death!

(Act II, sc. iv)

Long-Knife: the American.

GEORGE T. LANIGAN

1846–86

A Threnody

'The Ahkoond of Swat is dead.' – Press Dispatch

What, what, what,
What's the news from Swat?
    Sad news,
    Bad news,
Comes by the cable led
Through the Indian Ocean's bed,
Through the Persian Gulf, the Red
Sea and the Med-
Iterranean – he's dead;
The Ahkoond is dead!

For the Ahkoond I mourn.
    Who wouldn't?
He strove to disregard the message stern,
    But he Ahkoondn't.

Dead, dead, dead;
    Sorrow, Swats!
Swats wha' hae wi' Ahkoond bled,
Swats whom he had often led
Onward to a gory bed,
Or to victory,
    As the case might be.
    Sorrow, Swats!
Tears shed,
    Shed tears like water,
Your great Ahkoond is dead!
    That Swat's the matter!

Mourn, city of Swat!
Your great Ahkoond is not,
But lain 'mid worms to rot:
His mortal part alone, his soul was caught
(Because he was a good Ahkoond)

Up to the bosom of Mahound.
Though earthly walls his frame surround
(For ever hallowed be the ground!)
And sceptics mock the lowly mound
And say, 'He's now of no Ahkound!'
(His soul is in the skies!)
The azure skies that bend above his loved
    Metropolis of Swat
He sees with larger, other eyes,
Athwart all earthly mysteries –
    He knows what's Swat.

Let Swat bury the great Ahkoond
    With a noise of mourning and of lamentation!
Let Swat bury the great Ahkoond
    With the noise of the mourning of the Swattish nation!
    Fallen is at length
    Its tower of strength,
Its sun had dimmed ere it had nooned:
Dead lies the great Ahkoond,
    The great Ahkoond of Swat
    Is not.

ISABELLA VALANCY CRAWFORD

1850–87

True and False

Oh! spring was in his shining eyes
  And summer in his happy soul;
He bounded o'er the misty rise
  And saw the purple ocean roll.

With stars above and stars below,
  The lovely eve was fair as noon;
He saw above him richly glow
  The white shores of the sailing moon,

Her vales of jet, her pearly peaks,
  The lustre on her shining sands;
Leaped eager roses to his cheeks –
  He cried, 'I seek her silver strands!'

There rose a siren where the foam
  Of ocean sparkled most with stars:
She combed gold locks with golden comb;
  She floated past the murmuring bars.

She sang so loud, so silvery clear,
  The trees in far woods seemed to stir,
And seaward lean; from lake and mere
  Rushed eager rivers down to her.

She swept in mist of far blown hair,
  Star-white, from glittering steep to steep;
She loved his gay and dauntless air –
  Rose loftier from the purple deep,

Till, whiter than white coral rocks,
  She glimmered high against the moon.
And oh, she loved his raven locks!
  And oh, she sang him to his doom!

‘O boy, why dost thou upward turn
  The crystal of thy youthful eyes?
The true moon in the sea doth burn;
  Far ’neath my silver feet she lies.

‘Look down, look down, and thou shalt see
  A fairer moon and mellower stars;
A shadow pale and wan is she
  That floats o’er heaven’s azure bars.

’Look down, look down – the true moon lies
  Deep in mid-ocean’s fairest part;
Nor let that wan shade on the skies
  Draw all the tides of thy young heart.

‘O let mine arms thy neck entwine!
  Oh boy, come down to me, to me!
I’ll bring thee where the moon doth shine,
  The round moon in the silver sea.’

He heard the song, he felt the spell,
  He saw her white hand beckon on,
Believed the tale she sang so well,
  Beheld the moon that falsely shone.

The true moon wheeled her silver isle
  Serene in heaven’s blue mystery;
He sank in those white arms of guile
  To seek the false moon in the sea.

The Song of the Arrow
From *Gisli, the Chieftain*

What know I,
As I bite the blue veins of the throbbing sky,
To the quarry’s breast,
Hot from the sides of the sleek, smooth nest?

What know I
Of the will of the tense bow from which I fly?
What the need or jest
That feathers my flight to its bloody rest?

What know I
Of the will of the bow that speeds me on high?
What doth the shrill bow
Of the hand on its singing soul-string know?

Flame-swift speed I,
And the dove and the eagle shriek out and die.
Whence comes my sharp zest
For the heart of the quarry? The gods know best.

The Dark Stag

A startled stag, the blue-grey Night,
  Leaps down beyond black pines.
Behind – a length of yellow light –
  The hunter's arrow shines:
His moccasins are stained with red,
  He bends upon his knee,
From covering peaks his shafts are sped,
The blue mists plume his mighty head –
  Well may the swift Night flee!

The pale, pale Moon, a snow-white doe,
  Bounds by his dappled flank:
They beat the stars down as they go,
  Like wood-bells growing rank.
The winds lift dewlaps from the ground,
  Leap from the quaking reeds;
Their hoarse bays shake the forest round,
With keen cries on the track they bound —
  Swift, swift the dark stag speeds!

Away! his white doe, far behind,
  Lies wounded on the plain;
Yells at his flank the nimblest wind,
  His large tears fall in rain;
Like lily pads, small clouds grow white
  About his darkling way;

From his bald nest upon the height
The red-eyed eagle sees his flight;
He falters, turns, the antlered Night –
  The dark stag stands at bay!

His feet are in the waves of space;
  His antlers broad and dun
He lowers; he turns his velvet face
  To front the hunter, Sun;
He stamps the lilied clouds, and high
  His branches fill the west.
The lean stork sails across the sky,
The shy loon shrieks to see him die,
  The winds leap at his breast.

Roar the rent lakes as thro' the wave
  Their silver warriors plunge,
As vaults from core of crystal cave
  The strong, fierce muskallunge;
Red torches of the sumach glare,
  Fall's council-fires are lit;
The bittern, squaw-like, scolds the air;
The wild duck splashes loudly where
  The rustling rice-spears knit.

Shaft after shaft the red Sun speeds:
  Rent the stag's dappled side,
His breast, fanged by the shrill winds, bleeds,
  He staggers on the tide;
He feels the hungry waves of space
  Rush at him high and blue;
Their white spray smites his dusky face,
Swifter the Sun's fierce arrows race
  And pierce his stout heart thro'.

His antlers fall; once more he spurns
  The hoarse hounds of the day;
His blood upon the crisp blue burns,
  Reddens the mounting spray;
His branches smite the wave – with cries
  The loud winds pause and flag –

He sinks in space – red glow the skies,
The brown earth crimsons as he dies,
  The strong and dusky stag.

The Lily Bed

His cedar paddle, scented, red,
He thrust down through the lily bed;

Cloaked in a golden pause he lay,
Locked in the arms of the placid bay.

Trembled alone his bark canoe
As shocks of bursting lilies flew

Thro' the still crystal of the tide,
And smote the frail boat's birchen side;

Or, when beside the sedges thin
Rose the sharp silver of a fin;

Or when, a wizard swift and cold,
A dragon-fly beat out in gold

And jewels all the widening rings
Of water singing to his wings;

Or, like a winged and burning soul,
Dropped from the gloom an oriole

On the cool wave, as to the balm
Of the Great Spirit's open palm

The freed soul flies. And silence clung
To the still hours, as tendrils hung,

In darkness carven, from the trees,
Sedge-buried to their burly knees.

Stillness sat in his lodge of leaves;
Clung golden shadows to its eaves,

And on its cone-spiced floor, like maize,
Red-ripe, fell sheaves of knotted rays.

The wood, a proud and crested brave;
Bead-bright, a maiden, stood the wave.

And he had spoke his soul of love
With voice of eagle and of dove.

Of loud, strong pines his tongue was made;
His lips, soft blossoms in the shade,

That kissed her silver lips – hers cool
As lilies on his inmost pool –

Till now he stood, in triumph's rest,
His image painted in her breast.

One isle 'tween blue and blue did melt, –
A bead of wampum from the belt

Of Manitou – a purple rise
On the far shore heaved to the skies.

His cedar paddle, scented, red,
He drew up from the lily bed;

All lily-locked, all lily-locked,
His light bark in the blossoms rocked.

Their cool lips round the sharp prow sang,
Their soft clasp to the frail sides sprang,

With breast and lip they wove a bar.
Stole from her lodge the Evening Star;

With golden hand she grasped the mane
Of a red cloud on her azure plain.

It by the peaked, red sunset flew;
Cool winds from its bright nostrils blew.

They swayed the high, dark trees, and low
Swept the locked lilies to and fro.

With cedar paddle, scented, red,
He pushed out from the lily bed.

GEORGE FREDERICK CAMERON

1854–85

My Political Faith

I am not of those fierce, wild wills,
  Albeit from loins of warlike line,
  To wreck laws human and divine
Alike, that on a million ills
  I might erect one sacred shrine

To Freedom: nor again am I
  Of *these* who could be sold and bought
  To fall before a Juggernaut:
I hold all 'royal right' a lie –
  Save that a royal soul hath wrought!

It is in the extreme begins
  And ends all danger: if the Few
  Would feel, or if the Many knew
This fact, the mass of fewer sins
  Would shrive them in their passing through:

O'er all God's footstool not a slave
  Should under his great glory stand,
  For men would rise, swift sword in hand,
And give each tyrant to his grave
  And freedom to each lovely land.

Relics

Put them aside – I hate the sight of them! –
  That golden wonder from her golden hair –
  That faded lily which she once did wear
Upon her bosom – and that cold hard gem
  Which glittered on her taper finger fair.

They are of her, and, being so, they must
Be like to her, and she is all a lie
That seems a truth when truth is not a-nigh, –
A thing whose love is light as balance dust,
I loved her once, I love – nay, put them by!

Conceal them like the dead from sight away!
I must forget her and she was so dear
In former times! I could not bear them near:
Let them be sealed forever from the day –
Be wrapt in darkness, shrouded – buried here

Where never more my eye may rest on them!
This golden wonder from her golden hair –
This faded lily that she once did wear
Upon her bosom – and this joyless gem
That glittered on her taper finger fair.

Standing on Tiptoe

Standing on tiptoe ever since my youth
Striving to grasp the future just above,
I hold at length the only future – Truth,
And Truth is Love.

I feel as one who being awhile confined
Sees drop to dust about him all his bars:–
The clay grows less, and, leaving it, the mind
Dwells with the stars.

WILLIAM HENRY DRUMMOND

1854–1907

The Wreck of the 'Julie Plante'

A Legend of Lac St Pierre

On wan dark night on Lac St Pierre,
  De win' she blow, blow, blow,
An' de crew of de wood scow 'Julie Plante'
  Got scar't an' run below –
For de win' she blow lak hurricane
  Bimeby she blow some more,
An' de scow bus' up on Lac St Pierre
  Wan arpent from de shore.

De captinne walk on de fronte deck,
  An' walk de hin' deck too –
He call de crew from up de hole
  He call de cook also.
De cook she's name was Rosie,
  She come from Montreal,
Was chambre maid on lumber barge,
  On de Grande Lachine Canal.

De win' she blow from nor'-eas'-wes', –
  De sout' win' she blow too,
W'en Rosie cry 'Mon cher captinne,
  Mon cher, w'at I shall do?'
Den de Captinne t'row de big ankerre,
  But still de scow she dreef,
De crew he can't pass on de shore,
  Becos' he los' hees skeef.

De night was dark lak' wan black cat,
  De wave run high an' fas',
W'en de captinne tak' de Rosie girl
  An' tie her to de mas'.

Den he also tak' de life preserve,
  An' jomp off on de lak',
An' say, 'Good-bÿe, ma Rosie dear,
  I go drown for your sak'.'

Nex' morning very early
  'Bout ha'f-pas' two–t'ree–four –
De captinne – scow – an' de poor Rosie
  Was corpses on de shore,
For de win' she blow lak' hurricane
  Bimeby she blow some more,
An' de scow bus' up on Lac St Pierre,
  Wan arpent from de shore.

MORAL

Now all good wood scow sailor man
  Tak' warning by dat storm
An' go an' marry some nice French girl
  An' leev on wan beeg farm.
De win' can blow lak' hurricane
  An' s'pose she blow some more,
You can't get drown on Lac St Pierre
  So long you stay on shore.

WILFRED CAMPBELL

1858–1918

How One Winter Came in the Lake Region

For weeks and weeks the autumn world stood still,
  Clothed in the shadow of a smoky haze;
The fields were dead, the wind had lost its will,
And all the lands were hushed by wood and hill,
  In those grey, withered days.

Behind the blear sun rose and set,
  At night the moon would nestle in a cloud;
The fisherman, a ghost, did cast his net;
The lake its shores forgot to chafe and fret,
  And hushed its caverns loud.

Far in the smoky woods the birds were mute,
  Save that from blackened tree a jay would scream,
Or far in swamps, the lizard's lonesome lute
Would pipe in thirst, or by some gnarlèd root
  The tree-toad trilled his dream.

From day to day still hushed the season's mood,
  The streams stayed in their runnels shrunk and dry;
Suns rose aghast by wave and shore and wood,
And all the world, with ominous silence, stood
  In weird expectancy:

When one strange night the sun like blood went down,
  Flooding the heavens in a ruddy hue;
Red grew the lake, the sere fields parched and brown,
Red grew the marshes where the creeks stole down,
  But never a wind-breath blew.

That night I felt the winter in my veins,
  A joyous tremor of the icy glow;
And woke to hear the north's wild vibrant strains,
While far and wide, by withered woods and plains,
  Fast fell the driving snow.

*At Even**

I sit me moanless in the sombre fields,
The cows come with large udders down the dusk,
One cudless, the other chewing of a husk,
Her eye askance, for that athwart her heels,
Flea-haunted and rib-cavernous, there steals
The yelping farmer-dog. An old hen sits
And blinks her eyes. (Now I must rack my wits
To find a rhyme, while all this landscape reels.)
Yes! I forgot the sky. The stars are out,
There being no clouds; and then the pensive maid!
Of course she comes with tin-pail up the lane.
Mosquitoes hum and June bugs are about.
(That line hath 'quality' of loftiest grade.)
And I have eased my soul of its sweet pain.

* *Editor's note*: This is really a sonnet taken from the agricultural poems of John Pensive Bangs which Campbell stole and used as a filler for his column, 'At the Mermaid Inn', in the *Toronto Globe*. The poem appeared in the *Great Too-Too Magazine* for July 1893.

JOHN FREDERIC HERBIN

1860–1923

Haying

From the soft dyke-road, crooked and waggon-worn,
Comes the great load of rustling scented hay,
Slow-drawn with heavy swing and creaky sway
Through the cool freshness of the windless morn.
The oxen, yoked and sturdy, horn to horn,
Sharing the rest and toil of night and day,
Bend head and neck to the long hilly way
By many a season's labour marked and torn.
On the broad sea of dyke the gathering heat
Waves upward from the grass, where road on road
Is swept before the tramping of the teams.
And while the oxen rest beside the sweet
New hay, the loft receives the early load,
With hissing stir, among the dusty beams.

CHARLES G. D. ROBERTS

1860–1943

Marsyas

A little grey hill-glade, close-turfed, withdrawn
Beyond resort or heed of trafficking feet,
Ringed round with slim trunks of the mountain ash.
Through the slim trunks and scarlet bunches flash –
Beneath the clear chill glitterings of the dawn –
Far off, the crests, where down the rosy shore
The Pontic surges beat.
The plains lie dim below. The thin airs wash
The circuit of the autumn-coloured hills,
And this high glade, whereon
The satyr pipes, who soon shall pipe no more.
He sits against the beech-tree's mighty bole, –
He leans, and with persuasive breathing fills
The happy shadows of the slant-set lawn.
The goat-feet fold beneath a gnarlèd root;
And sweet, and sweet the note that steals and thrills
From slender stops of that shy flute.
Then to the goat-feet comes the wide-eyed fawn
Hearkening; the rabbits fringe the glade, and lay
Their long ears to the sound;
In the pale boughs the partridge gather round,
And quaint hern from the sea-green river reeds;
The wild ram halts upon a rocky horn
O'erhanging; and, unmindful of his prey,
The leopard steals with narrowed lids to lay
His spotted length along the ground.
The thin airs wash, the thin clouds wander by,
And those hushed listeners move not. All the morn
He pipes, soft-swaying, and with half-shut eye,
In rapt content of utterance, –
nor heeds
The young god standing in his branchy place,
The languor on his lips, and in his face,
Divinely inaccessible, the scorn.

Canada

O Child of Nations, giant-limbed,
  Who stand'st among the nations now
Unheeded, unadorned, unhymned,
  With unanointed brow, –

How long the ignoble sloth, how long
  The trust in greatness not thine own?
Surely the lion's brood is strong
  To front the world alone!

How long the indolence, ere thou dare
  Achieve thy destiny, seize thy fame, –
Ere our proud eyes behold thee bear
  A nation's franchise, nation's name?

The Saxon force, the Celtic fire,
  These are thy manhood's heritage!
Why rest with babes and slaves? Seek higher
  The place of race and age.

I see to every wind unfurled
  The flag that bears the Maple Wreath;
Thy swift keels furrow round the world
  Its blood-red folds beneath;

Thy swift keels cleave the furthest seas;
  Thy white sails swell with alien gales;
To stream on each remotest breeze
  The black smoke of thy pipes exhales.

O Falterer, let thy past convince
  Thy future, – all the growth, the gain,
The fame since Cartier knew thee, since
  Thy shores beheld Champlain!

Montcalm and Wolfe! Wolfe and Montcalm!
  Quebec, thy storied citadel
Attest in burning song and psalm
  How here thy heroes fell!

O Thou that bor'st the battle's brunt
  At Queenston and at Lundy's Lane, –

On whose scant ranks but iron front
  The battle broke in vain! –

Whose was the danger, whose the day,
  From whose triumphant throats the cheers,
At Chrysler's Farm, at Chateauguay,
  Storming like clarion-bursts our ears?

On soft Pacific slopes, – beside
  Strange floods that northward rave and fall, –
Where chafes Acadia's chainless tide –
  Thy sons await thy call.

They wait; but some in exile, some
  With strangers housed, in stranger lands, –
And some Canadian lips are dumb
  Beneath Egyptian sands.

O mystic Nile! Thy secret yields
  Before us; thy most ancient dreams
Are mixed with far Canadian fields
  And murmur of Canadian streams.

But thou, my country, dream not thou!
  Wake, and behold how night is done, –
How on thy breast, and o'er thy brow,
  Bursts the uprising sun!

Three Sonnets
From *Songs of the Common Day*

The Pea-fields

These are the fields of light, and laughing air,
  And yellow butterflies, and foraging bees,
  And whitish, wayward blossoms winged as these,
And pale green tangles like a seamaid's hair.
Pale, pale the blue, but pure beyond compare,
  And pale the sparkle of the far-off seas,
  A-shimmer like these fluttering slopes of peas,
And pale the open landscape everywhere.

From fence to fence a perfumed breath exhales
  O'er the bright pallor of the well-loved fields, –
My fields of Tantramar in summer-time;
  And, scorning the poor feed their pasture yields,
Up from the bushy lots the cattle climb,
  To gaze with longing through the grey, mossed rails.

The Herring Weir

Back to the green deeps of the outer bay
  The red and amber currents glide and cringe,
  Diminishing behind a luminous fringe
Of cream-white surf and wandering wraiths of spray.
Stealthily, in the old reluctant way,
  The red flats are uncovered, mile on mile,
  To glitter in the sun a golden while.
Far down the flats, a phantom sharply grey,
The herring weir emerges, quick with spoil.
  Slowly the tide forsakes it. Then draws near,
  Descending from the farm-house on the height,
A cart, with gaping tubs. The oxen toil
  Sombrely o'er the level to the weir,
  And drag a long black trail across the light.

The Flight of the Geese

I hear the low wind wash the softening snow,
  The low tide loiter down the shore. The night
  Full filled with April forecast, hath no light.
The salt wave on the sedge-flat pulses slow.
Through the hid furrows lisp in murmurous flow
  The thaw's shy ministers; and hark! The height
  Of heaven grows weird and loud with unseen flight
Of strong hosts prophesying as they go!

High through the drenched and hollow night their wings
  Beat northward hard on winter's trail. The sound
Of their confused and solemn voices, borne
Athwart the dark to their long Arctic morn,
  Comes with a sanction and an awe profound,
A boding of unknown, foreshadowed things.

At Tide Water

The red and yellow of the Autumn salt-grass,
  The grey flats, and the yellow-grey full tide,
The lonely stacks, the grave expanse of marshes, –
  O Land wherein my memories abide,
I have come back that you may make me tranquil,
  Resting a little at your heart of peace,
Remembering much amid your serious leisure,
  Forgetting more amid your large release.
For yours the wisdom of the night and morning,
  The word of the inevitable years,
The open heaven's unobscured communion,
  And the dim whisper of the wheeling spheres.
The great things and the terrible I bring you,
  To be illumined in your spacious breath, –
Love, and the ashes of desire, and anguish,
  Strange laughter, and the unhealing wound of death.
These in the world, all these, have come upon me,
  Leaving me mute and shaken with surprise.
Oh, turn them in your measureless contemplation,
  And in their mastery teach me to be wise.

In the Night Watches

When the little spent winds are at rest in the tamarack tree
In the still of the night,
And the moon in her waning is wan and misshapen,
And out on the lake
The loon floats in a glimmer of light,
And the solitude sleeps, –
Then I lie in my bunk wide awake,
And my long thoughts stab me with longing,
Alone in my shack by the marshes of lone Margaree.

Far, oh so far in the forests of silence they lie,
The lake and the marshes of lone Margaree,
And no man comes my way.
Of spruce logs my cabin is builded securely;
With slender spruce saplings its bark roof is battened down surely;
In its rafters the mice are at play,
With rustlings furtive and shy,
In the still of the night.

Awake, wide-eyed, I watch my window-square,
Pallid and grey.
(O Memory, pierce me not! O Longing, stab me not!
O ache of longing memory, pass me by, and spare,
And let me sleep!)
Once and again the loon cries from the lake.
Though no breath stirs
The ghostly tamaracks and the brooding firs,
Something as light as air leans on my door.

Is it an owl's wing brushes at my latch?
Are they of foxes, those light feet that creep
Outside, light as fall'n leaves
On the forest floor?
From the still lake I hear
A feeding trout rise to some small night fly.
The splash, how sharply clear!
Almost I see the wide, slow ripple circling to the shore.

The spent winds are at rest. But my heart, spent and faint, is unresting.
Long, long a stranger to peace . . .
O so Dear, O so Far, O so Unforgotten-in-dream,
Somewhere in the world, somewhere beyond reach of my questing.
Beyond seas, beyond years,
You will hear my heart in your sleep, and you will stir restlessly;
You will stir at the touch of my hand on your hair;
You will wake with a start,
With my voice in your ears
And an old, old ache at your heart,
(In the still of the night)
And your pillow wet with tears.

The Aim

O Thou who lovest not alone
The swift success, the instant goal,
But hast a lenient eye to mark
The failures of the inconstant soul,

Consider not my little worth, –
The mean achievement, scamped in act,
The high resolve and low result,
The dream that durst not face the fact.

But count the reach of my desire.
Let this be something in Thy sight: –
I have not, in the slothful dark,
Forgot the Vision and the Height.

Neither my body nor my soul
To earth's low ease will yield consent.
I praise Thee for my will to strive.
I bless Thy goad of discontent.

ARCHIBALD LAMPMAN

1861–99

Heat

From plains that reel to southward, dim,
  The road runs by me white and bare;
Up the steep hill it seems to swim
  Beyond, and melt into the glare.
Upward half way, or it may be
  Nearer the summit, slowly steals
A hay-cart, moving dustily
  With idly clacking wheels.

By his cart's side the wagoner
  Is slouching slowly at his ease,
Half-hidden in the windless blur
  Of white dust puffing to his knees.
This wagon on the height above,
From sky to sky on either hand,
Is the sole thing that seems to move
  In all the heat-held land.

Beyond me in the fields the sun
  Soaks in the grass and hath his will;
I count the marguerites one by one;
  Even the buttercups are still.
On the brook yonder not a breath
Disturbs the spider or the midge.
The water-bugs draw close beneath
  The cool gloom of the bridge.

Where the far elm-tree shadows flood
  Dark patches in the burning grass,
The cows, each with her peaceful cud,
  Lie waiting for the heat to pass.
From somewhere on the slope near by
  Into the pale depth of the noon
A wandering thrush slides leisurely
  His thin revolving tune.

In intervals of dreams I hear
  The cricket from the droughty ground;
The grass-hoppers spin into mine ear
  A small innumerable sound.
I lift mine eyes sometimes to gaze:
  The burning sky-line blinds my sight:
The woods far off are blue with haze:
  The hills are drenched in light.

And yet to me not this or that
  Is always sharp or always sweet;
In the sloped shadow of my hat
  I lean at rest, and drain the heat;
Nay more, I think some blessèd power
  Hath brought me wandering idly here:
In the full furnace of this hour
  My thoughts grow keen and clear.

Life and Nature

I passed through the gates of the city,
  The streets were strange and still,
Through the doors of the open churches
  The organs were moaning shrill.

Through the doors and the great high windows
  I heard the murmur of prayer,
And the sound of their solemn singing
  Streamed out on the sunlit air,

A sound of some great burden
  That lay on the world's dark breast,
Of the old, and the sick, and the lonely,
  And the weary that cried for rest.

I strayed through the midst of the city
  Like one distracted or mad.
'Oh, Life! Oh, Life!' I kept saying,
  And the very word seemed sad.

I passed through the gates of the city,
And I heard the small birds sing,
I laid me down in the meadows
Afar from the bell-ringing.

In the depth and the bloom of the meadows
I lay on the earth's quiet breast,
The poplar fanned me with shadows,
And the veery sang me to rest.

Blue, blue was the heaven above me,
And the earth green at my feet;
'Oh, Life! Oh, Life!' I kept saying,
And the very word seemed sweet.

September

Now hath the summer reached her golden close,
And, lost amid her corn-fields, bright of soul,
Scarcely perceives from her divine repose
How near, how swift, the inevitable goal:
Still, still, she smiles, though from her careless feet
The bounty and the fruitful strength are gone,
And through the soft long wondering days goes on
The silent sere decadence sad and sweet.

The kingbird and the pensive thrush are fled,
Children of light, too fearful of the gloom;
The sun falls low, the secret word is said,
The mouldering woods grow silent as the tomb;
Even the fields have lost their sovereign grace,
The cone-flower and the marguerite; and no more,
Across the river's shadow-haunted floor,
The paths of skimming swallows interlace.

Already in the outland wilderness
The forests echo with unwonted dins;
In clamorous gangs the gathering woodmen press
Northward, and the stern winter's toil begins.

Around the long low shanties, whose rough lines
  Break the sealed dreams of many an unnamed lake,
  Already in the frost-clear morns awake
The crash and thunder of the falling pines.

Where the tilled earth, with all its fields set free,
  Naked and yellow from the harvest lies,
By many a loft and busy granary,
  The hum and tumult of the thrashers rise;
There the tanned farmers labor without slack,
  Till twilight deepens round the spouting mill,
  Feeding the loosened sheaves, or with fierce will,
Pitching waist-deep upon the dusty stack.

Still a brief while, ere the old year quite pass,
  Our wandering steps and wistful eyes shall greet
The leaf, the water, the belovèd grass;
  Still from these haunts and this accustomed seat
I see the wood-wrapt city, swept with light,
  The blue long-shadowed distance, and, between,
  The dotted farm-lands with their parcelled green,
The dark pine forest and the watchful height.

I see the broad rough meadow stretched away
  Into the crystal sunshine, wastes of sod,
Acres of withered vervain, purple-grey,
  Branches of aster, groves of goldenrod;
And yonder, toward the sunlit summit, strewn
  With shadowy boulders, crowned and swathed with weed,
  Stand ranks of silken thistles, blown to seed,
Long silver fleeces shining like the noon.

In far-off russet corn-fields, where the dry
  Gray shocks stand peaked and withering, half concealed
In the rough earth, the orange pumpkins lie,
  Full-ribbed; and in the windless pasture-field
The sleek red horses o'er the sun-warmed ground
  Stand pensively about in companies,
  While all around them from the motionless trees
The long clean shadows sleep without a sound.

Under the cool elm-trees floats the distant stream,
  Moveless as air; and o'er the vast warm earth
The fathomless daylight seems to stand and dream,
  A liquid cool elixir – all its girth
Bound with faint haze, a frail transparency,
  Whose lucid purple barely veils and fills
  The utmost valleys and the thin last hills,
Nor mars one whit their perfect clarity.

Thus without grief the golden days go by,
  So soft we scarcely notice how they wend,
And like a smile half happy, or a sigh,
  The summer passes to her quiet end;
And soon, too soon, around the cumbered eaves
  Sly frosts shall take the creepers by surprise,
  And through the wind-touched reddening woods shall rise
October with the rain of ruined leaves.

Solitude

How still it is here in the woods. The trees
  Stand motionless, as if they do not dare
  To stir, lest it should break the spell. The air
Hangs quiet as spaces in a marble frieze.
Even this little brook, that runs at ease,
  Whispering and gurgling in its knotted bed,
  Seems but to deepen with its curling thread
Of sound the shadowy sun-pierced silences.

Sometimes a hawk screams or a woodpecker
  Startles the stillness from its fixèd mood
With his loud careless tap. Sometimes I hear
  The dreamy white-throat from some far-off tree
Pipe slowly on the listening solitude
  His five pure notes succeeding pensively.

A Summer Evening

The clouds grow clear, the pine-wood glooms and stills
With brown reflections in the silent bay,
And far beyond the pale blue-misted hills
The rose and purple evening dreams away.
The thrush, the veery, from mysterious dales
Rings his last round; and outward like a sea
The shining, shadowy heart of heaven unveils
The starry legend of eternity.
The day's long troubles lose their sting and pass.
Peaceful the world, and peaceful grows my heart.
The gossip cricket from the friendly grass
Talks of old joys and takes the dreamer's part.
Then night, the healer, with unnoticed breath,
And sleep, dark sleep, so near, so like to death.

Winter Evening

To-night the very horses springing by
Toss gold from whitened nostrils. In a dream
The streets that narrow to the westward gleam
Like rows of golden palaces; and high
From all the crowded chimneys tower and die
A thousand aureoles. Down in the west
The brimming plains beneath the sunset rest,
One burning sea of gold. Soon, soon shall fly
The glorious vision, and the hours shall feel
A mightier master; soon from height to height,
With silence and the sharp unpitying stars,
Stern creeping frosts, and winds that touch like steel,
Out of the depth beyond the eastern bars,
Glittering and still shall come the awful night.

Among the Orchards

Already in the dew-wrapped vineyards dry
Dense weights of heat press down. The large bright drops
Shrink in the leaves. From dark acacia tops
The nut-hatch flings his short reiterate cry;
And even as the sun mounts hot and high
Thin voices crowd the grass. In soft long strokes
The wind goes murmuring through the mountain oaks.
Faint wefts creep out along the blue and die.
I hear far in among the motionless trees –
Shadows that sleep upon the shaven sod –
The thud of dropping apples. Reach on reach
Stretch plots of perfumed orchard, where the bees
Murmur among the full-fringed goldenrod
Or cling half-drunken to the rotting peach.

Midnight

From where I sit, I see the stars,
And down the chilly floor
The moon between the frozen bars
Is glimmering dim and hoar.

Without in many a peakèd mound
The glinting snowdrifts lie;
There is no voice or living sound;
The embers slowly die.

Yet some wild thing is in mine ear;
I hold my breath and hark;
Out of the depth I seem to hear
A crying in the dark:

No sound of man or wife or child,
No sound of beast that groans,
Or of the wind that whistles wild,
Or of the tree that moans:

I know not what it is I hear;
  I bend my head and hark:
I cannot drive it from mine ear,
  That crying in the dark.

Snow

White are the far-off plains, and white
  The fading forests grow;
The wind dies out along the height,
  And denser still the snow,
A gathering weight on roof and tree,
  Falls down scarce audibly.

The road before me smooths and fills
  Apace, and all about
The fences dwindle, and the hills
  Are blotted slowly out;
The naked trees loom spectrally
  Into the dim white sky

The meadows and far-sheeted streams
  Lie still without a sound;
Like some soft minister of dreams
  The snow-fall hoods me round;
In wood and water, earth and air,
  A silence everywhere.

Save when at lonely intervals
  Some farmer's sleigh, urged on,
With rustling runners and sharp bells,
  Swings by me and is gone;
Or from the empty waste I hear
  A sound remote and clear;

The barking of a dog, or call
  To cattle, sharply pealed,
Borne echoing from some wayside stall
  Or barnyard far afield;

Then all is silent, and the snow
  Falls, settling soft and slow.

The evening deepens, and the gray
  Folds closer earth and sky;
The world seems shrouded far away;
  Its noises sleep, and I,
As secret as yon buried stream,
  Plod dumbly on, and dream.

The City of the End of Things

Beside the pounding cataracts
Of midnight streams unknown to us
'Tis builded in the leafless tracts
And valleys huge of Tartarus.
Lurid and lofty and vast it seems;
It hath no rounded name that rings,
But I have heard it called in dreams
The City of the End of Things.

Its roofs and iron towers have grown
None knoweth how high within the night,
But in its murky streets far down
A flaming terrible and bright
Shakes all the stalking shadows there,
Across the walls, across the floors,
And shifts upon the upper air
From out a thousand furnace doors;
And all the while an awful sound
Keeps roaring on continually,
And crashes in the ceaseless round
Of a gigantic harmony.
Through its grim depths re-echoing
And all its weary height of walls,
With measured roar and iron ring,
The inhuman music lifts and falls.
Where no thing rests and no man is,

And only fire and night hold sway;
The beat, the thunder and the hiss
Cease not, and change not, night nor day.

And moving at unheard commands,
The abysses and vast fires between,
Flit figures that with clanking hands
Obey a hideous routine;
They are not flesh, they are not bone,
They see not with the human eye,
And from their iron lips is blown
A dreadful and monotonous cry;
And whoso of our mortal race
Should find that city unaware,
Lean Death would smite him face to face,
And blanch him with its venomed air:
Or caught by the terrific spell,
Each thread of memory snapt and cut,
His soul would shrivel and its shell
Go rattling like an empty nut.

It was not always so, but once,
In days that no man thinks upon,
Fair voices echoed from its stones,
The light above it leaped and shone:
Once there were multitudes of men,
That built that city in their pride,
Until its might was made, and then
They withered age by age and died.
But now of that prodigious race,
Three only in an iron tower,
Set like carved idols face to face,
Remain the masters of its power;
And at the city gate a fourth,
Gigantic and with dreadful eyes,
Sits looking toward the lightless north,
Beyond the reach of memories;
Fast rooted to the lurid floor,
A bulk that never moves a jot,
In his pale body dwells no more,
Or mind or soul, – an idiot!

But sometime in the end those three
Shall perish and their hands be still,
And with the master's touch shall flee
Their incommunicable skill.
A stillness absolute as death
Along the slacking wheels shall lie,
And, flagging at a single breath,
The fires that moulder out and die.
The roar shall vanish at its height,
And over that tremendous town
The silence of eternal night
Shall gather close and settle down.
All its grim grandeur, tower and hall,
Shall be abandoned utterly,
And into rust and dust shall fall
From century to century;
Nor ever living thing shall grow,
Nor trunk of tree, nor blade of grass;
No drop shall fall, no wind shall blow,
Nor sound of any foot shall pass:
Alone of its accursèd state,
One thing the hand of Time shall spare,
For the grim Idiot at the gate
Is deathless and eternal there.

BLISS CARMAN

1861–1929

Low Tide on Grand Pré

The sun goes down, and over all
  These barren reaches by the tide
Such unelusive glories fall,
  I almost dream they yet will bide
  Until the coming of the tide.

And yet I know that not for us,
  By any ecstasy of dream,
He lingers to keep luminous
  A little while the grievous stream,
  Which frets, uncomforted of dream –

A grievous stream, that to and fro
  Athrough the fields of Acadie
Goes wandering, as if to know
  Why one beloved face should be
  So long from home and Acadie.

Was it a year or lives ago
  We took the grasses in our hands,
And caught the summer flying low
  Over the waving meadow lands,
  And held it there between our hands?

The while the river at our feet –
  A drowsy inland meadow stream –
At set of sun the after-heat
  Made running gold, and in the gleam
  We freed our birch upon the stream.

There down along the elms at dusk
  We lifted dripping blade to drift,
Through twilight scented fine like musk,
  Where night and gloom awhile uplift,
  Nor sunder soul and soul adrift.

And that we took into our hands
  Spirit of life or subtler thing –
Breathed on us there, and loosed the bands
  Of death, and taught us, whispering,
  The secret of some wonder-thing.

Then all your face grew light, and seemed
  To hold the shadow of the sun;
The evening faltered, and I deemed
  That time was ripe, and years had done
  Their wheeling underneath the sun.

So all desire and all regret,
  And fear and memory, were naught;
One to remember or forget
  The keen delight our hands had caught;
  Morrow and yesterday were naught.

The night has fallen, and the tide . . .
  Now and again comes drifting home,
Across these aching barrens wide,
  A sigh like driven wind or foam:
  In grief the flood is bursting home.

A Northern Vigil

Here by the gray north sea,
  In the wintry heart of the wild,
Comes the old dream of thee,
  Guendolen, mistress and child.

The heart of the forest grieves
  In the drift against my door;
A voice is under the eaves,
  A footfall on the floor.

Threshold, mirror and hall,
  Vacant and strangely aware,
Wait for their soul's recall
  With the dumb expectant air.

Here when the smouldering west
  Burns down into the sea,
I take no heed of rest
  And keep the watch for thee.

I sit by the fire and hear
  The restless wind go by,
On the long dirge and drear,
  Under the low bleak sky.

When day puts out to sea
  And night makes in for land,
There is no lock for thee,
  Each door awaits thy hand!

When night goes over the hill
  And dawn comes down the dale,
It's O for the wild sweet will
  That shall no more prevail!

When the zenith moon is round,
  And snow-wraiths gather and run,
And there is set no bound
  To love beneath the sun,

O wayward will, come near
  The old mad wilful way,
The soft mouth at my ear
  With words too sweet to say!

Come, for the night is cold,
  The ghostly moonlight fills
Hollow and rift and fold
  Of the eerie Ardise hills!

The windows of my room
  Are dark with bitter frost,
The stillness aches with doom
  Of something loved and lost.

Outside, the great blue star
  Burns in the ghostland pale,
Where giant Algebar
  Holds on the endless trail.

Come, for the years are long,
  And silence keeps the door,
Where shapes with the shadows throng
  The firelit chamber floor.

Come, for thy kiss was warm,
  With the red embers' glare
Across thy folding arm
  And dark tumultuous hair!

And though thy coming rouse
  The sleep-cry of no bird,
The keepers of the house
  Shall tremble at thy word.

Come, for the soul is free!
  In all the vast dreamland
There is no lock for thee,
  Each door awaits thy hand.

Ah, not in dreams at all,
  Fleering, perishing, dim,
But thy old self, supple and tall,
  Mistress and child of whim!

The proud imperious guise,
  Impetuous and serene,
The sad mysterious eyes,
  And dignity of mien!

Yea, wilt thou not return,
  When the late hill-winds veer,
And the bright hill-flowers burn
  With the reviving year?

When April comes, and the sea
  Sparkles as if it smiled,
Will they restore to me
  My dark Love, empress and child?

The curtains seem to part;
  A sound is on the stair,
As if at the last . . . I start;
  Only the wind is there.

Lo, now far on the hills
   The crimson fumes uncurled,
Where the caldron mantles and spills
   Another dawn on the world!

A Seamark

A Threnody for Robert Louis Stevenson

Cold, the dull cold! What ails the sun,
And takes the heart out of the day?
What makes the morning look so mean,
The Common so forlorn and gray?

The wintry city's granite heart
Beats on in iron mockery,
And like the roaming mountain rains,
I hear the thresh of feet go by.

It is the lonely human surf
Surging through alleys chill with grime,
The muttering churning ceaseless floe
Adrift out of the North of time.

Fades, it all fades! I only see
The poster with its reds and blues
Bidding the heart stand still to take
Its desolating stab of news.

That intimate and magic name:
'Dead in Samoa.' . . . Cry your cries,
O city of the golden dome,
Under the gray Atlantic skies!

But I have wander-biddings now.
Far down the latitudes of sun,
An island mountain of the sea,
Piercing the green and rosy zone,

Goes up into the wondrous day.
And there the brown-limbed island men
Are bearing up for burial,
Within the sun's departing ken,

The master of the roving kind.
And there where time will set no mark
For his irrevocable rest,
Under the spacious melting dark,

With all the nomad tented stars
About him, they have laid him down
Above the crumbling of the sea,
Beyond the turmoil of renown.

O all you hearts about the world
In whom the truant gipsy blood,
Under the frost of this pale time,
Sleeps like the daring sap and flood

That dream of April and reprieve!
You whom the haunted vision drives,
Incredulous of home and ease,
Perfection's lovers all your lives!

You whom the wander-spirit loves
To lead by some forgotten clue
Forever vanishing beyond
Horizon brinks forever new;

The road, unmarked, ordained, whereby
Your brothers of the field and air
Before you, faithful, blind and glad,
Emerged from chaos pair by pair;

The road whereby you too must come,
In the unvexed and fabled years
Into the country of your dream,
With all your knowledge in arrears!

You who can never quite forget
Your glimpse of Beauty as she passed,
The well-head where her knee was pressed,
The dew wherein her foot was cast;

O you who bid the paint and clay
Be glorious when you are dead,
And fit the plangent words in rhyme
Where the dark secret lurks unsaid;

You brethren of the light-heart guild,
The mystic fellowcraft of joy,
Who tarry for the news of truth,
And listen for some vast ahoy

Blown in from sea, who crowd the wharves
With eager eyes that wait the ship
Whose foreign tongue may fill the world
With wondrous tales from lip to lip;

Our restless loved adventurer,
On secret orders come to him,
Has slipped his cable, cleared the reef,
And melted on the white sea-rim.

O granite hills, go down in blue!
And like green clouds in opal calms,
You anchored islands of the main,
Float up your loom of feathery palms!

For deep within your dales, where lies
A valiant earthling stark and dumb,
This savage undiscerning heart
Is with the silent chiefs who come

To mourn their kin and bear him gifts, –
Who kiss his hand, and take their place,
This last night he receives his friends,
The journey-wonder on his face.

He 'was not born for age'. Ah no,
For everlasting youth is his!
Part of the lyric of the earth
With spring and leaf and blade he is.

'Twill nevermore be April now
But there will lurk a thought of him
At the street corners, gay with flowers
From rainy valleys purple-dim.

O chiefs, you do not mourn alone!
In that stern North where mystery broods,
Our mother grief has many sons
Bred in those iron solitudes.

It does not help them, to have laid
Their coil of lightning under seas;
They are as impotent as you
To mend the loosened wrists and knees.

And yet how many a harvest night,
When the great luminous meteors flare
Along the trenches of the dusk,
The men who dwell beneath the Bear,

Seeing those vagrants of the sky
Float through the deep beyond their hark,
Like Arabs through the wastes of air, –
A flash, a dream, from dark to dark, –

Must feel the solemn large surmise:
By a dim vast and perilous way
We sweep through undetermined time,
Illumining this quench of clay,

A moment staunched, then forth again.
Ah, not alone you climb the steep
To set your loving burden down
Against the mighty knees of sleep.

With you we hold the sombre faith
Where creeds are sown like rain at sea;
And leave the loveliest child of earth
To slumber where he longed to be.

His fathers lit the dangerous coast
To steer the daring merchant home;
His courage lights the dark'ning port
Where every sea-worn sail must come.

And since he was the type of all
That strain in us which still must fare,
The fleeting migrant of a day,
Heart-high, outbound for otherwhere,

Now therefore, where the passing ships
Hand on the edges of the noon,
And Northern liners trail their smoke
Across the rising yellow moon.

Bound for his home, with shuddering screw
That beats its strength out into speed,
Until the pacing watch descries
On the sea-line a scarlet seed

Smolder and kindle and set fire
To the dark selvedge of the night,
The deep blue tapestry of stars,
Then sheet the dome in pearly light,

There in perpetual tides of day,
Where men may praise him and deplore,
The place of his lone grave shall be
A seamark set forevermore,

High on a peak adrift with mist,
And round whose bases, far beneath
The snow-white wheeling tropic birds,
The emerald dragon breaks his teeth.

Christmas Song

Above the weary waiting world,
Asleep in chill despair,
There breaks a sound of joyous bells
Upon the frosted air.
And o'er the humblest rooftree, lo,
A star is dancing on the snow.

What makes the yellow star to dance
Upon the brink of night?
What makes the breaking dawn to glow
So magically bright, –
And all the earth to be renewed
With infinite beatitude?

The singing bells, the throbbing star,
The sunbeams on the snow,
And the awakening heart that leaps
New ecstasy to know, –
They all are dancing in the morn
Because a little child is born.

From *Sappho*

XCIII

When in the spring the swallows all return,
And the bleak bitter sea grows mild once more
With all its thunders softened to a sigh;

When to the meadows the young green comes back,
And swelling buds put forth on every bough,
With wild-wood odours on the delicate air;

Ah, then, in that so lovely earth wilt thou
With all thy beauty love me all one way,
And make me all thy lover as before?

Lo, where the white-maned horses of the surge,
Plunging in thunderous onset to the shore,
Trample and break and charge along the sand!

Vestigia

I took a day to search for God,
And found Him not. But as I trod
By rocky ledge, through woods untamed,
Just where one scarlet lily flamed,
I saw His footprint in the sod.

Then suddenly, all unaware,
Far off in the deep shadows, where
A solitary hermit thrush
Sang through the holy twilight hush –
I heard His voice upon the air.

And even as I marvelled how
God gives us Heaven here and now,
In a stir of wind that hardly shook
The poplar leaves beside the brook –
His hand was light upon my brow.

At last with evening as I turned
Homeward, and thought what I had learned
And all that there was still to probe –
I caught the glory of His robe
Where the last fires of sunset burned.

Back to the world with quickening start
I looked and longed for any part
In making saving Beauty be . . .
And from that kindling ecstasy
I knew God dwelt within my heart.

FREDERICK GEORGE SCOTT

1861–1944

The Sting of Death

'Is Sin, then, fair?'
  Nay, love, come now,
Put back the hair
  From his sunny brow;
See, here, blood-red
Across his head
A brand is set,
The word – 'Regret.'

'Is Sin so fleet
  That while he stays,
Our hands and feet
  May go his ways?'
Nay, love, his breath
Clings round like death,
He slakes desire
With liquid fire.

'Is Sin Death's sting?'
  Ay, sure he is,
His golden wing
  Darkens man's bliss;
And when Death comes,
Sin sits and hums
A chaunt of fears
Into man's ears.

'How slayeth Sin?'
  First, God is hid,
And the heart within
  By its own self child;
Then the maddened brain
Is scourged by pain
To sin as before
And more and more,
  For evermore.

Crucifixion

Lord, must I bear the whole of it, or none?
'Even as I was crucified, My son.'

Will it suffice if I the thorn-crown wear?
'To take the scourge My shoulders were made bare.'

My hands, O Lord, must I be pierced in both?
'Twain gave I to the hammer, nothing loth.'

But surely, Lord, my feet need not be nailed?
'Had Mine not been, then love had not prevailed.'

What need I more, O Lord, to fill my part?
'Only the spear-point in thy broken heart.'

PAULINE JOHNSON

1861–1913

The Corn Husker

Hard by the Indian lodges, where the bush
  Breaks in a clearing, through ill-fashioned fields,
She comes to labour, when the first still hush
  Of autumn follows large and recent yields.

Age in her fingers, hunger in her face,
  Her shoulders stooped with weight of work and years,
But rich in tawny colouring of her race,
  She comes a-field to strip the purple ears.

And all her thoughts are with the days gone by,
  Ere might's injustice banished from their lands
Her people, that to-day unheeded lie,
  Like the dead husks that rustle through her hands.

DUNCAN CAMPBELL SCOTT

1862–1947

The Piper of Arll

There was in Arll a little cove
Where the salt wind came cool and free:
A foamy beach that one would love,
If he were longing for the sea.

A brook hung sparkling on the hill,
The hill swept far to ring the bay;
The bay was faithful, wild or still,
To the heart of the ocean far away.

There were three pines above the comb
That, when the sun flared and went down,
Grew like three warriors reaving home
The plunder of a burning town.

A piper lived within the grove,
Tending the pasture of his sheep;
His heart was swayed with faithful love,
From the springs of God's ocean clear and deep.

And there a ship one evening stood,
Where ship had never stood before;
A pennon bickered red as blood,
An angel glimmered at the prore.

About the coming on of dew,
The sails burned rosy, and the spars
Were gold, and all the tackle grew
Alive with ruby-hearted stars.

The piper heard an outland tongue,
With music in the cadenced fall;
And when the fairy lights were hung,
The sailors gathered one and all,

And leaning on the gunwales dark,
Crusted with shells and dashed with foam,
With all the dreaming hills to hark,
They sang their longing songs of home.

When the sweet airs had fled away,
The piper, with a gentle breath,
Moulded a tranquil melody
Of lonely love and long-for death.

When the fair sound began to lull,
From out the fireflies and the dew,
A silence held the shadowy hull,
Until the eerie tune was through.

Then from the dark and dreamy deck
An alien song began to thrill;
It mingled with the drumming beck,
And stirred the braird upon the hill.

Beneath the stars each sent to each
A message tender, till at last
The piper slept upon the beach,
The sailors slumbered round the mast.

Still as a dream till nearly dawn,
The ship was bosomed on the tide;
The streamlet, murmuring on and on,
Bore the sweet water to her side.

Then shaking out her lawny sails,
Forth on the misty sea she crept;
She left the dawning of the dales,
Yet in his cloak the piper slept.

And when he woke he saw the ship,
Limned black against the crimson sun;
Then from the disc he saw her slip,
A wraith of shadow – she was gone.

He threw his mantle on the beach,
He went apart like one distraught,
His lips were moved – his desperate speech
Stormed his inviolable thought.

He broke his human-throated reed,
And threw it in the idle rill;
But when his passion had its mead,
He found it in the eddy still.

He mended well the patient flue,
Again he tried its varied stops;
The closures answered right and true,
And starting out in piercing drops,

A melody began to drip
That mingled with a ghostly thrill
The vision-spirit of the ship,
The secret of his broken will.

Beneath the pines he piped and swayed,
Master of passion and of power;
He was his soul and what he played,
Immortal for a happy hour.

He, singing into nature's heart,
Guiding his will by the world's will,
With deep, unconscious, childlike art
Had sung his soul out and was still.

And then at evening came the bark
That stirred his dreaming heart's desire;
It burned slow lights along the dark
That died in glooms of crimson fire.

The sailors launched a sombre boat,
And bent with music at the oars;
The rhythm throbbing every throat,
And lapsing round the liquid shores,

Was that true tune the piper sent,
Unto the wave-worn mariners,
When with the beck and ripple blent
He heard that outland song of theirs.

Silent they rowed him, dip and drip,
The oars beat out an exequy,
They laid him down within the ship,
They loosed a rocket to the sky.

It broke in many a crimson sphere
That grew to gold and floated far,
And left the sudden shore-line clear,
With one slow-changing, drifting star.

Then out they shook the magic sails,
That charmed the wind in other seas,
From where the west line pearls and pales,
They waited for a ruffling breeze.

But in the world there was no stir,
The cordage slacked with never a creak,
They heard the flame begin to purr
Within the lantern at the peak.

They could not cry, they could not move,
They felt the lure from the charmed sea;
They could not think of home or love
Or any pleasant land to be.

They felt the vessel dip and trim,
And settle down from list to list;
They saw the sea-plain heave and swim
As gently as a rising mist.

And down so slowly, down and down,
Rivet by rivet, plank by plank;
A little flood of ocean flown
Across the deck, she sank and sank.

From knee to breast the water wore,
It crept and crept; ere they were ware
Gone was the angel at the prore,
They felt the water float their hair.

They saw the salt plain spark and shine
They threw their faces to the sky;
Beneath a deepening film of brine
They saw the star-flash blur and die.

She sank and sank by yard and mast,
Sank down the shimmering gradual dark;
A little drooping pennon last
Showed like the black fin of a shark.

And down she sank till, keeled in sand,
She rested safely balanced true,
With all her upward gazing band,
The piper and the dreaming crew.

And there, unmarked of any chart,
In unrecorded deeps they lie,
Empearled within the purple heart
Of the great sea for aye and aye.

Their eyes are ruby in the green
Long shaft of sun that spreads and rays,
And upward with a wizard sheen
A fan of sea-light leaps and plays.

Tendrils of or and azure creep,
And globes of amber light are rolled,
And in the glooming of the deep
Their eyes are starry pits of gold.

And sometimes in the liquid night
The hull is changed, a solid gem,
That glows with a soft stony light,
The lost prince of a diadem.

And at the keel a vine is quick,
That spreads its bines and works and weaves
O'er all the timbers veining thick
A plenitude of silver leaves.

Thoughts

These thoughts of mine
Oh! would they were away.
Thoughts that have progress
Give me stay
And eagerness for life;
But these dead thoughts

Hang like burned forests
By a northern lake,
Whose waters take
The bone-grey skeletons
And mirror the grey bones,
Both dead, the trees and the reflections.

Compare these thoughts
To anything that nothing tells, –
To toads alive for centuries in stone cells,
To a styleless dial on a fiery lawn,
To the trapped bride within the oaken chest,
Or to the dull, intolerable bells
That beat the dawn
And will not let us rest!

Watkwenies

Vengeance was once her nation's lore and law:
When the tired sentry stooped above the rill,
Her long knife flashed, and hissed, and drank its fill;
Dimly below her dripping wrist she saw
One wild hand, pale as death and weak as straw,
Clutch at the ripple in the pool; while shrill
Sprang through the dreaming hamlet on the hill,
The war-cry of the triumphant Iroquois.

Now clothed with many an ancient flap and fold,
And wrinkled like an apple kept till May,
She weighs the interest-money in her palm,
And when the Agent calls her valiant name,
Hears, like the war-whoops of her perished day,
The lads playing snow-snake in the stinging cold.

The Onondaga Madonna

She stands full-throated and with careless pose,
This woman of a weird and waning race,
The tragic savage lurking in her face,
Where all her pagan passion burns and glows;
Her blood is mingled with her ancient foes,
And thrills with war and wildness in her veins;
Her rebel lips are dabbled with the stains
Of feuds and forays and her father's woes.

And closer in the shawl about her breast,
The latest promise of her nation's doom,
Paler than she her baby clings and lies,
The primal warrior gleaming from his eyes;
He sulks, and burdened with his infant gloom,
He draws his heavy brows and will not rest.

The Sailor's Sweetheart

O if love were had for asking
  In the markets of the town,
Hardly a lass would think to wear
  A fine silken gown:
But love is had by grieving
By choosing and by leaving,
And there's no one now to ask me
If heavy lies my heart.

O if love were had for a deep wish
  In the deadness of the night,
There'd be a truce to longing
  Between the dusk and the light:
But love is had for sighing,
For living and for dying,
And there's no one now to ask me
If heavy lies my heart.

O if love were had for taking
  Like honey from the hive,
The bees that made the tender stuff
  Could hardly keep alive:
But love it is a wounded thing,
A tremor and a smart,
And there's no one left to kiss me now
Over my heavy heart.

A Song

In the air there are no coral-
  Reefs or ambergris,
No rock-pools that hide the lovely
  Sea-anemones,
No strange forms that flow with phosphor
  In a deep-sea night,
No slow fish that float their colour
  Through the liquid light,
No young pearls, like new moons, growing
  Perfect in their shells;
If you be in search of beauty
  Go where beauty dwells.

In the sea there are no sunsets
  Crimson in the west,
No dark pines that hold the shadow
  On the mountain-crest,
There is neither mist nor moonrise
  Rainbows nor rain,
No sweet flowers that in the autumn
  Die to bloom again,
Music never moves the silence, –
  Reeds or silver bells;
If you be in search of beauty
  Go where beauty dwells.

At Delos

An iris-flower with topaz leaves,
  With a dark heart of deeper gold,
Died over Delos when light failed
  And the night grew cold.

No wave fell mourning in the sea
  Where age on age beauty had died;
For that frail colour withering away
  No sea-bird cried.

There is no grieving in the world
  As beauty fades throughout the years:
The pilgrim with the weary heart
  Brings to the grave his tears.

TOM MacINNES

1867–1951

Zalinka

1

Last night in a land of triangles,
  I lay in a cubicle, where
A girl in pyjamas and bangles
  Slept with her hands in my hair.

2

I wondered if either or neither
  Of us were properly there,
Being subject to queer aberrations –
Astral and thin aberrations –
  Which leave me no base to compare:
  No adequate base to compare:
Tho' her hands, with their wristful of bangles,
  Were certainly fast in my hair,
While the moon made pallid equations
  Thro' a delicate window there.

3

I was glad that she slept for I never
  Can tell what the finish will be:
What enamoured, nocturnal endeavour
  May end in the killing of me:
But, in the moonlit obscuro
  Of that silken, somniferous lair,
Like a poet consumed with a far lust
  Of things unapproachably fair
I fancied her body of stardust –
Pounded of spices and stardust –
  Out of the opulent air.

4

Then the moon, with its pale liquidations,
  Fell across her in argentine bars,
And I thought: This is fine – but to-morrow
  What cut of Dawn's cold scimitars
Will sever my hold on this creature –
  I mean of this creature on me? –
Amorous creature of exquisite aura –
  Marvel of dark glamorie.

5

What joy of folly then followed
  Is beyond my expression in rhyme:
And I do not expect you to grasp it
  When I speak of expansions of time:
Of reaching and zooming serenely
  As it were at right angles to time:
Knowing well you will think, on your level,
  This was only a dream indiscreet –
  Or experience quite indiscreet:
But little I care, in this instance,
  What you do or do not think discreet:
  O utterance futile, but sweet,
  Like a parrot I pause and repeat,
In delight of my own, and for nothing,
  To myself I repeat and repeat:

6

Last night in a land of triangles,
  I lay in a cubicle where
A girl in pyjamas and bangles
  Slept with her hands in my hair.

JOHN McCRAE

1872–1918

In Flanders Fields

In Flanders fields the poppies blow
Between the crosses, row on row,
  That mark our place; and in the sky
  The larks, still bravely singing, fly
Scarce heard amid the guns below.

We are the Dead. Short days ago
We lived, felt dawn, saw sunset glow,
  Loved and were loved, and now we lie,
      In Flanders fields.

Take up our quarrel with the foe:
To you from failing hands we throw
  The torch; be yours to hold it high.
  If ye break faith with us who die
We shall not sleep, though poppies grow
      In Flanders fields.

VIRNA SHEARD

d. 1943

The Yak

For hours the princess would not play or sleep
  Or take the air;
Her red mouth wore a look it meant to keep
  Unmelted there;
(Each tired courtier longed to shriek, or weep,
  But did not dare.)

Then one young duchess said: 'I'll to the King,
  And short and flat
I'll say, "Her Highness will not play or sing
  Or pet the cat;
Or feed the peacocks, or do anything –
  And that is that."'

So to the King she went, curtsied, and said,
  (No whit confused):
'Your Majesty, I would go home! The court is dead.
  Have me excused;
The little princess still declines,' – she tossed her head –
  'To be amused.'

Then to the princess stalked the King: 'What ho!' he roared,
  'What may you lack?
Why do you look, my love, so dull and bored
  With all this pack
Of minions?' She answered, while he waved his sword:
  'I want a yak.'

'A yak!' he cried (each courtier cried, 'Yak! Yak!'
  As at a blow)
'Is that a figure on the zodiac?
  Or horse? Or crow?'
The princess sadly said to him: 'Alack
  I do not know.'

'We'll send the vassals far and wide, my dear!'
  Then quoth the King:
'They'll make a hunt for it, then come back here
  And bring the thing; –
But warily, – lest it be wild, or queer,
  Or have a sting.'

So off the vassals went, and well they sought
  On every track,
Till by and by in old Tibet they bought
  An ancient yak.
Yet when the princess saw it, she said naught
  But: 'Take it back!'

And what the courtiers thought they did not say
  (Save soft and low),
For that is surely far the wisest way
  As we all know;
While for the princess? She went back to play!
          Tra-rill-a-la-lo!
          Tra-rill-a-la-lo!
          Tra-rill-a-la-lo!

Exile

Ben-Arabie was the Camel,
  Belonging to the Zoo.
He lived there through a dozen years,
  With nothing much to do,
But chew, and chew, and chew, and chew,
  And chew, and chew, and chew.

He wondered when he might go home, –
  And what they kept him for;
Because he hated Zooish sounds
  And perfumes – more and more; –
Decidedly he hated them
  Much more, and more, and more.

And why the world turned white and cold
He did not understand.
He only wanted lots of sun
And lots and lots of sand;
Just sand, and sand, and sand, and sand,
And sand, and sand, and sand.

He longed to see an Arab Sheik,
And Arab girls and boys;
The kind of noise he yearned for most
Was plain Arabian noise;
(The sound of little drums and flutes
And all that sort of noise.)

He leant against the wind to hear
The sound of harness bells;
He sniffed the air for scent of spice
The nomad merchant sells;
He dreamed of pleasant tinkling bells,
Of spice and tinkling bells.

The keepers said that he grew queer.
They wondered why he sighed;
They called him supercilious
And crabbed and sun-dried;
(Indeed he was quite crabbed and
Exceedingly sun-dried.)

But ere his woolly fur was gone
They put him on a train –
For a rich old Arab bought him
And sent him home again; –
O joyous day! He sent him home;
He sent him home again!

ROBERT SERVICE

1874–1958

The Shooting of Dan McGrew

A bunch of the boys were whooping it up in the Malamute saloon;
The kid that handles the music-box was hitting a rag-time tune;
Back of the bar, in a solo game, sat Dangerous Dan McGrew,
And watching his luck was his light-o'-love, the lady that's known as Lou.

When out of the night, which was fifty below, and into the din and the glare,
There stumbled a miner fresh from the creeks, dog-dirty, and loaded for bear.
He looked like a man with a foot in the grave, and scarcely the strength of a louse,
Yet he tilted a poke of dust on the bar, and he called for drinks for the house.
There was none could place the stranger's face, though we searched ourselves for a clue;
But we drank his health, and the last to drink was Dangerous Dan McGrew.

There's men that somehow just grip your eyes, and hold them hard like a spell;
And such was he, and he looked to me like a man who had lived in hell;
With a face most hair, and the dreary stare of a dog whose day is done,
As he watered the green stuff in his glass, and the drops fell one by one.
Then I got to figgering who he was, and wondering what he'd do,
And I turned my head – and there watching him was the lady that's known as Lou.

His eyes went rubbering round the room, and he seemed in a kind of daze,
Till at last that old piano fell in the way of his wandering gaze.
The rag-time kid was having a drink; there was no one else on the stool,
So the stranger stumbles across the room, and flops down there like a fool.
In a buckskin shirt that was glazed with dirt he sat, and I saw him sway;
Then he clutched the keys with his talon hands – my God! but that man could play!

Were you ever out in the Great Alone, when the moon was awful clear,
And the icy mountains hemmed you in with a silence you most could *hear*;
With only the howl of a timber wolf, and you camped there in the cold,
A half-dead thing in a stark, dead world, clean mad for the muck called gold;
While high overhead, green, yellow and red, the North Lights swept in bars –
Then you've a hunch what the music mean . . . hunger and night and the stars.

And hunger not of the belly kind, that's banished with bacon and beans;
But the gnawing hunger of lonely men for a home and all that it means;
For a fireside far from the cares that are, four walls and a roof above;
But oh! so cramful of cosy joy, and crowned with a woman's love;
A woman dearer than all the world, and true as Heaven is true –
(God! how ghastly she looks through her rouge, – the lady that's known as Lou).

Then on a sudden the music changed, so soft that you scarce
  could hear;
But you felt that your life had been looted clean of all that it
  once held dear;
That someone had stolen the woman you loved; that her love
  was a devil's lie;
That your guts were gone, and the best for you was to crawl
  away and die.
'Twas the crowning cry of a heart's despair, and it thrilled
  you through and through –
'I guess I'll make it a spread misere,' said Dangerous Dan
  McGrew.

The music almost died away . . . then it burst like a pent-up
  flood;
And it seemed to say, 'Repay, repay,' and my eyes were blind
  with blood.
The thought came back of an ancient wrong, and it stung like
  a frozen lash,
And the lust awoke to kill, to kill . . . then the music stopped
  with a crash.

And the stranger turned, and his eyes they burned in a most
  peculiar way;
In a buckskin shirt that was glazed with dirt he sat, and I saw
  him sway;
Then his lips went in in a kind of grin, and he spoke, and his
  voice was calm;
And, 'Boys,' says he, 'you don't know me, and none of you
  care a damn;
But I want to state, and my words are straight, and I'll bet
  my poke they're true,
That one of you is a hound of hell . . . and that one is Dan
  McGrew.'

Then I ducked my head, and the lights went out, and two
guns blazed in the dark;
And a woman screamed, and the lights went up, and two
men lay stiff and stark;
Pitched on his head, and pumped full of lead, was Dangerous
Dan McGrew,
While the man from the creeks lay clutched to the breast of
the lady that's known as Lou.

These are the simple facts of the case, and I guess I ought to
know;
They say that the stranger was crazed with 'hooch', and I'm
not denying it's so.
I'm not so wise as the lawyer guys, but strictly between us
two –
The woman that kissed him and – pinched his poke – was the
lady that's known as Lou.

THEODORE GOODRIDGE ROBERTS

1877–1953

The Blue Heron

In a green place lanced through
With amber and gold and blue;
A place of water and weeds
And roses pinker than dawn,
And ranks of lush young reeds,
And grasses straightly withdrawn
From graven ripples of sands,
The still blue heron stands.

Smoke-blue he is, and grey
As embers of yesterday.
Still he is, as death;
Like stone, or shadow of stone,
Without a pulse or breath,
Motionless and alone
There in the lily stems:
But his eyes are alive like gems.

Still as a shadow; still
Grey feather and yellow bill:
Still as an image made
Of mist and smoke half hid
By windless sunshine and shade,
Save when a yellow lid
Slides and is gone like a breath:
Death-still – and sudden as death!

The Wreckers' Prayer

In the old days before the building of the lighthouses, the poor 'noddies' of many a Newfoundland outport prayed for wrecks – aye, and with easy consciences. Only the few hundreds of them who took to deep-sea voyaging ever learned anything of the world and its peoples. All the world excepting their own desolate bays and 'down Nort'', was 'up-along' to them . . . a grand, rich place where all men were gentlemen wearing collars and coats, eating figgy-duff every day and smoking all they wanted to. The folk of up-along had the easy end of life; so why shouldn't they contribute something of their goods and gear to poor but honest noddies now and then, even if against their inclinations – aye, even if at the cost of their lives?

Give us a wrack or two, Good Lard,
For winter in Tops'il Tickle bes hard,
Wid grey frost creepin' like mortal sin
And perishin' lack of bread in the bin.

A grand, rich wrack, us do humbly pray,
Busted abroad at the break o' day
An' hove clear in 'crost Tops'il Reef,
Wid victuals an' gear to beguile our grief.

God of reefs an' tides an' sky,
Heed Ye our need an' hark to our cry!
Bread by the bag an' beef by the cask,
Ease for sore bellies bes all we ask.

One grand wrack – or maybe two? –
Wid gear an' victuals to see us through
'Til Spring starts up like the leap of day
An' the fish strike back into Tops'il Bay.

One rich wrack – for Thy hand bes strong!
A barque or a brig from up along
Bemused by Thy twisty tides, O Lard!
For winter in Tops'il Tickle bes hard.

Loud an' long will us sing Yer praise,
Marciful Fadder, O Ancient of Days,
Master of fog an' tide an' reef!
Heave us a wrack to beguile our grief. Amen.

MARJORIE PICKTHALL

1883–1922

Père Lalement

I lift the Lord on high,
Under the murmuring hemlock boughs, and see
The small birds of the forest lingering by
And making melody.
These are mine acolytes and these my choir,
And this mine altar in the cool green shade,
Where the wild soft-eyed does draw nigh
Wondering, as in the byre
Of Bethlehem the oxen heard Thy cry
And saw Thee, unafraid.

My boatmen sit apart,
Wolf-eyed, wolf-sinewed, stiller than the trees.
Help me, O Lord, for very slow of heart
And hard of faith are these.
Cruel are they, yet Thy children. Foul are they,
Yet wert Thou born to save them utterly.
Then make me as I pray
Just to their hates, kind to their sorrows, wise
After their speech, and strong before their free
Indomitable eyes.

Do the French lilies reign
Over Mont Royal and Stadacona still?
Up the St Lawrence comes the spring again,
Crowning each southward hill
And blossoming pool with beauty, while I roam
Far from the perilous folds that are my home,
There where we built St Ignace for our needs,
Shaped the rough roof tree, turned the first sweet sod,
St Ignace and St Louis, little beads
On the rosary of God.

Pines shall Thy pillars be,
Fairer than those Sidonian cedars brought
By Hiram out of Tyre, and each birch-tree
Shines like a holy thought.
But come no worshippers; shall I confess,
St Francis-like, the birds of the wilderness?
O, with Thy love my lonely head uphold.
A wandering shepherd I, who hath no sheep;
A wandering soul, who hath no scrip, nor gold,
Nor anywhere to sleep.

My hour of rest is done;
On the smooth ripple lifts the long canoe;
The hemlocks murmur sadly as the sun
Slants his dim arrows through.
Whither I go I know not, nor the way,
Dark with strange passions, vexed with heathen charms,
Holding I know not what of life or death;
Only be Thou beside me day by day,
Thy rod my guide and comfort, underneath
Thy everlasting arms.

Mary Tired

Through the starred Judean night
  She went in travail of the Light:
  With the earliest hush she saw
God beside her in the straw.
One small taper glimmered clear,
  Drowsing Joseph nodded near;
All the glooms were rosed with wings.
She that knew the Spirit's kiss
Wearied of the bright abyss.
She was tired of heavenly things.
There between the day and night
These she counted for delight:
Baby kids that butted hard
  In the shadowy stable yard;
  Silken doves that dipped and preened

Where the crumbling well-curb greened;
Sparrows in the vine, and small
Sapphired flies upon the wall,
So lovely they seemed musical.
  In the roof a swallow built;
All the newborn airs were spilt
Out of cups the morning made
Of a glory and a shade.
These her solemn eyelids felt,
While unseen the seraphs knelt.
Then a young mouse, sleek and bold,
Rustling in the winnowed gold,
To her shadow crept, and curled
Near the Ransom of the World.

On Amaryllis
A Tortoyse

My name was Amaryllis. I
From a harde Shell put forthe to fly;
No Bird, alas! with Beautie prim'd,
Hath Death th' inconstant Fowler lim'd.
No antick Moth on blossoms set
Hath Judgement taken in a Net.
So dull, so slowe, so meeke I went
In my House-Roof that pay'd no Rent,
E'en my deare Mistresse guess'd no Spark
Could e'er enlight'n my dustie Dark.
  Judge not, ye Proud. Each lowlie Thing
  May lack the Voyce, not Heart, to sing.
  The Worme that from the Moulde suspires
  May be attun'd with heavenlie Quires,
  And I, a-crawling in my Straw,
  Was moved by Love, and made by Law.
  So all ye wise, who 'neath your Clod
  Go creeping onwards up to God,
  Take Heart of me, who by His Grace,
  Slough'd off my Pris'n and won my Race.

Quiet

Come not the earliest petal here, but only
Wind, cloud, and star,
Lovely and far,
Make it less lonely.

Few are the feet that seek her here, but sleeping
Thoughts sweet as flowers
Linger for hours,
Things winged, yet weeping.

Here in the immortal empire of the grasses,
Time, like one wrong
Note in a song,
With their bloom, passes.

E. J. PRATT

1883–1964

Come Away, Death

Willy-nilly, he comes or goes, with the clown's logic,
Comic in epitaph, tragic in epithalamium,
And unseduced by any mused rhyme.
However blow the winds over the pollen,
Whatever the course of the garden variables,
He remains the constant,
Ever flowering from the poppy seeds.

There was a time he came in formal dress,
Announced by Silence tapping at the panels
In deep apology.
A touch of chivalry in his approach,
He offered sacramental wine,
And with acanthus leaf
And petals of the hyacinth
He took the fever from the temples
And closed the eyelids,
Then led the way to his cool longitudes
In the dignity of the candles.

His mediaeval grace is gone –
Gone with the flame of the capitals
And the leisured turn of the thumb
Leafing the manuscripts,
Gone with the marbles
And the Venetian mosaics,
With the bend of the knee
Before the rose-strewn feet of the Virgin.
The *paternosters* of his priests,
Committing clay to clay,
Have rattled in their throats
Under the gride of his traction tread.

One night we heard his footfall – one September night –
In the outskirts of a village near the sea.

There was a moment when the storm
Delayed its fist, when the surf fell
Like velvet on the rocks – a moment only;
The strangest lull we ever knew!
A sudden truce among the oaks
Released their fratricidal arms;
The poplars straightened to attention
As the winds stopped to listen
To the sound of a motor drone –
And then the drone was still.
We heard the tick-tock on the shelf,
And the leak of valves in our hearts.
A calm condensed and lidded
As at the core of a cyclone ended breathing.
This was the monologue of Silence
Grave and unequivocal.

What followed was a bolt
Outside the range and target of the thunder,
And human speech curved back upon itself
Through Druid runways and the Piltdown scarps,
Beyond the stammers of the Java caves,
To find its origins in hieroglyphs
On mouths and eyes and cheeks
Etched by a foreign stylus never used
On the outmoded page of the Apocalypse.

From *Brébeuf and His Brethren*

The fury of taunt was followed by fury of blow.
Why did not the flesh of Brébeuf cringe to the scourge,
Respond to the heat, for rarely the Iroquois found
A victim that would not cry out in such pain – yet here
The fire was on the wrong fuel. Whenever he spoke,
It was to rally the soul of his friend whose turn
Was to come through the night while the eyes were uplifted in
  prayer,
Imploring the Lady of Sorrows, the mother of Christ,
As pain brimmed over the cup and the will was called

To stand the test of the coals. And sometimes the speech
Of Brébeuf struck out, thundering reproof to his foes,
Half-rebuke, half-defiance, giving them roar for roar.
Was it because the chancel became the arena,
Brébeuf a lion at bay, not a lamb on the altar,
As if the might of a Roman were joined to the cause
Of Judaea? Speech they could stop for they girdled his lips,
But never a moan could they get. Where was the source
Of his strength, the home of his courage that topped the best
Of their braves and even out-fabled the lore of their legends?
In the bunch of his shoulders which often had carried a load
Extorting the envy of guides at an Ottawa portage?
The heat of the hatchets was finding a path to that source.
In the thews of his thighs which had mastered the trails of the
Neutrals?
They would gash and beribbon those muscles. Was it the blood?
They would draw it fresh from its fountain. Was it the heart?
They dug for it, fought for the scraps in the way of the wolves.
But not in these was the valour or stamina lodged;
Nor in the symbol of Richelieu's robes or the seals
Of Mazarin's charters, nor in the stir of the *lilies*
Upon the Imperial folds; nor yet in the words
Loyola wrote on a table of lava-stone
In the cave of Manresa – not in these the source –
But in the sound of invisible trumpets blowing
Around two slabs of board, right-angled, hammered
By Roman nails and hung on a Jewish hill.

From *The Titanic*

Out on the water was the same display
Of fear and self-control as on the deck –
Challenge and hesitation and delay,
The quick return, the will to save, the race
Of snapping oars to put the realm of space
Between the half-filled lifeboats and the wreck.

. . . Aboard the ship, whatever hope of dawn
Gleamed from the *Carpathia*'s riding lights was gone,

For every knot was matched by each degree
Of list. The stern was lifted bodily
When the bow had sunk three hundred feet, and set
Against the horizon stars in silhouette
Were the blade curves of the screws, hump of the rudder.
The downward pull and after buoyancy
Held her a minute poised but for a shudder
That caught her frame as with the upward stroke
Of the sea a boiler or a bulkhead broke.

Climbing the ladders, gripping shroud and stay,
Storm-rail, ringbolt or fairlead, every place
That might befriend the clutch of hand or brace
Of foot, the fourteen hundred made their way
To the heights of the aft decks, crowding the inches
Around the docking bridge and cargo winches.
And now that last salt tonic which had kept
The valour of the heart alive – the bows
Of the immortal seven that had swept
The strings to outplay, outdie their orders, ceased.
Five minutes more, the angle had increased
From eighty on to ninety when the rows
Of deck and porthole lights went out, flashed back
A brilliant second and again went black.
Another bulkhead crashed, then following
The passage of the engines as they tore
From their foundations, taking everything
Clean through the bows from 'midships with a roar
Which drowned all cries upon the deck and shook
The watchers in the boats, the liner took
Her thousand fathoms journey to her grave.

* * *

And out there in the starlight, with no trace
Upon it of its deed but the last wave
From the *Titanic* fretting at its base,
Silent, composed, ringed by its icy broods,
The gray shape with the palaeolithic face
Was still the master of the longitudes.

The Prize Cat

Pure blood domestic, guaranteed,
Soft-mannered, musical in purr,
The ribbon had declared the breed,
Gentility was in the fur.

Such feline culture in the gads,
No anger ever arched her back –
What distance since those velvet pads
Departed from the leopard's track!

And when I mused how Time had thinned
The jungle strains within the cells,
How human hands had disciplined
Those prowling optic parallels;

I saw the generations pass
Along the reflex of a spring,
A bird had rustled in the grass,
The tab had caught it on the wing:

Behind the leap so furtive-wild
Was such ignition in the gleam,
I thought an Abyssinian child
Had cried out in the whitethroat's scream.

From Stone to Steel

From stone to bronze, from bronze to steel
Along the road-dust of the sun,
Two revolutions of the wheel
From Java to Geneva run.

The snarl Neanderthal is worn
Close to the smiling Aryan lips,
The civil polish of the horn
Gleams from our praying finger tips.

The evolution of desire
Has but matured a toxic wine,
Drunk long before its heady fire
Reddened Euphrates or the Rhine.

Between the temple and the cave
The boundary lies tissue-thin:
The yearlings still the altars crave
As satisfaction for a sin.

The road goes up, the road goes down –
Let Java or Geneva be –
But whether to the cross or crown,
The path lies through Gethsemane.

Come Not the Seasons Here

Comes not the springtime here,
  Though the snowdrop came,
And the time of the cowslip is near,
  For a yellow flame
Was found in a tuft of green;
  And the joyous shout
  Of a child rang out
That a cuckoo's eggs were seen.

Comes not the summer here,
  Though the cowslip be gone,
Though the wild rose blow as the year
  Draws faithfully on;
Though the face of the poppy be red
  In the morning light,
  And the ground be white
With the bloom of the locust shed.

Comes not the autumn here,
  Though someone said
He found a leaf in the sere
  By an aster dead;
And knew that the summer was done,
  For a herdsman cried
That his pastures were brown in the sun,
  And his wells were dried.

Nor shall the winter come,
  Though the elm be bare,
And every voice be dumb
  On the frozen air;
But the flap of a waterfowl
  In the marsh alone,
Or the hoot of a horned owl
  On a glacial stone.

KENNETH LESLIE

1892–1974

Two Sonnets
From *By Stubborn Stars*

I

The silver herring throbbed thick in my seine,
silver of life, life's silver sheen of glory;
my hands, cut with the cold, hurt with the pain
of hauling the net, pulled the heavy dory,
heavy with life, low in the water, deep
plunged to the gunwale's lips in the stress of rowing,
the pulse of rowing that puts the world to sleep,
world within world endlessly ebbing, flowing.
At length you stood on the landing and you cried,
with quick low cries you timed me stroke on stroke
as I steadily won my way with the fulling tide
and crossed the threshold where the last wave broke
and coasted over the step of water and threw
straight through the air my mooring line to you.

II

A warm rain whispers, but the earth knows best
and turns a deaf ear, waiting for the snow,
the foam of bloom forgotten, the rolling crest
of green forgotten and the fruit swelling slow.
The shearing plow was here and cut the mould
and shouldered over the heavy rain-soaked lands,
letting the hot breath out for the quiet cold
to reach deep down with comfort in its hands.
The sap is ebbing from the tips of the trees
to the dry and secret heart, hiding away
from the blade still green with stubborn memories;
down in the roots it closes the door of clay
on grief and growing and this late warm rain
babbling false promises in the pasture lane.

W. W. E. ROSS

1894–1966

The Walk

He walked through the woods
and saw the merging
of the tall trunks
in the green distance, –
the undergrowth
of mottled green,
with sunlight and shadow,
and flowers starting

here and there
on the mottled ground;
he looked along
the green distance
and up towards
the greenly-laden
curving boughs
of the tall trees;

and down a slope,
as he walked onward
down the sloping
ground, he saw
in among
the green, broken,
the blue shimmering
of lake-water.

Fish

A fish dripping
sparkling drops
of crystal water,
pulled from the lake;

long has it dwelt
in the cool water,
in the cold water
of the lake.

Long has it wandered
to and fro
over the bottom
of the lake
among mysterious
recesses
there in the semi-
light of the water;

now to appear
surprised, aghast,
out of its element
into the day; –
out of the cold
and shining lake
the fish dripping
sparkling water.

The Diver

I would like to dive
Down
Into this still pool
Where the rocks at the bottom are safely deep,

Into the green
Of the water seen from within,
A strange light
Streaming past my eyes –

Things hostile,
You cannot stay here, they seem to say;
The rocks, slime-covered, the undulating
Fronds of weeds –

And drift slowly
Among the cooler zones;
Then, upward turning,
Break from the green glimmer

Into the light,
White and ordinary of the day,
And the mild air,
With the breeze and the comfortable shore.

'The saws were shrieking'

The saws were shrieking
and cutting into
the clean white wood
of the spruce logs
or the tinted hemlock
that smells as sweet –
or stronger pine,
the white and the red.

A whirling saw
received the logs;
the sound was ominous
and shrill,
rising above
the duller roaring
of the mill's
machinery.

From the revolving
of the saw
came slices of clear wood,
newly sawn,
white pine and red,
or spruce and hemlock,
the sweet spruce,
and the sweet hemlock.

In the Ravine

In the ravine I stood
and watched the snowflakes
falling into the stream
            into the stream
flowing gracefully between
banks of snow
                        The black water
of the winter creek came
around a bend above
and disappeared
around a bend below

Filled with melted snow
to the brim
the creek came
around a bend –
and disappeared below
around a bend –
ground covered with snow

Thus I stood the snow
descended by degrees
into the stream
            into the stream

RAYMOND KNISTER

1899–1932

The Plowman

All day I follow
Watching the swift dark furrow
That curls away before me,
And care not for skies or upturned flowers,
And at the end of the field
Look backward
Ever with discontent.
A stone, a root, a strayed thought
Has warped the line of that furrow –
And urge my horses 'round again.

Sometimes even before the row is finished
I must look backward;
To find, when I come to the end
That there I swerved.

Unappeased I leave the field,
Expectant, return.

The horses are very patient.
When I tell myself
This time
The ultimate unflawed turning
Is before my share,
They must give up their rest.

Someday, someday, be sure,
I shall turn the furrow of all my hopes
But I shall not, doing it, look backward.

Feed

For Danny whistling slowly
'Down in Tennessee'

A fat white shoat by the trough
Lifts his snout a moment to hear,
Among the guzzling and slavering comrades,
Squeezing and forcing:
And begins to feed again.
Whenever the certain note comes
He will raise his jaws
With his unturning eyes,
Then lean again to scoop up the swill.

Lake Harvest

Down on the flat of the lake
Out on the slate and the green,
Spotting the border of Erie's sleeping robe of silver-blue changeable silk,
In sight of the shimmer of silver-blue changeable silk,
In the sun,
The men are sawing the frosted crystal.
Patient the horses look on from the sleighs,
Patient the trees, down from the bank, darkly ignoring the sun.
Each saw swings and whines in a grey-mittened hand,
And diamonds and pieces of a hundred rainbows are strown around.

Nell

From *A Row of Stalls*

Nellie Rakerfield
Came from an estate in Scotland,
Two years old, and won a championship.
It was not her fault that her foals
Were few, and mostly died or were runted.
She worked every day when she raised them,
Never was tired of dragging her
Nineteen hundred pounds

About the farm and the roads, with
Great loads behind it.
She never kicked, bit, nor crowded
In the stall,
Was always ready at a chirp
And seemed to have forgotten delicate care.

But the day they hitched her
To the corpse of her six-months-old colt,
She tried to run away, half way to the bush.
She never seemed quite so willing, afterward.
But the colt was too heavy.

The Roller

The trees still seem a reincarnation
Though the ground is dried and hard.
Hear, a mile away,
The tenor bellow of a roller
As it strikes the furrows.
The short corn will bend, to be sure,
But the soil will be flattened,
And rain on the broken lumps
Shall work an alchemy.

There is only the creak of harness
And the low words of teamsters
In the unplanted fields,
And in the field where the roller sounds
There shall be no more loudness
Until the wind rasps dried stalks
And boys shout to each other
Above the crisp surf-noise,
Among gold mounds of corn
Stretching in rows.

F. R. SCOTT

b. 1899

Trans Canada

Pulled from our ruts by the made-to-order gale
We sprang upward into a wider prairie
And dropped Regina below like a pile of bones.

Sky tumbled upon us in waterfalls,
But we were smarter than a Skeena salmon
And shot our silver body over the lip of air
To rest in a pool of space
On the top storey of our adventure.

A solar peace
And a six-way choice.

Clouds, now, are the solid substance,
A floor of wool roughed by the wind
Standing in waves that halt in their fall.
A still of troughs.

The plane, our planet,
Travels on roads that are not seen or laid
But sound in instruments on pilots' ears,
While underneath,
The sure wings
Are the everlasting arms of science.

Man, the lofty worm, tunnels his latest clay,
And bores his new career.

This frontier, too, is ours.
This everywhere whose life can only be led
At the pace of a rocket
Is common to man and man,
And every country below is an I land.

The sun sets on its top shelf,
And stars seem farther from our nearer grasp.
I have sat by nights beside a cold lake

And touched things smoother than moonlight on still water,
But the moon on this cloud sea is not human,
And here is no shore, no intimacy,
Only the start of space, the road to suns.

A Grain of Rice

Such majestic rhythms, such tiny disturbances.
The rain of the monsoon falls, an inescapable treasure,
    hundreds of millions live
Only because of the certainty of this season,
    The turn of the wind.

The frame of our human house rests on the motion
Of earth and of moon, the rise of continents,
Invasion of deserts, erosion of hills,
    The capping of ice.

Today, while Europe tilted, drying the Baltic,
I read of a battle between brothers in anguish,
    A flag moved a mile.

And today, from a curled leaf cocoon, in the course of its
    rhythm,
I saw the break of a shell, the creation
Of a great Asian moth, radiant, fragile,
Incapable of not being born, and trembling
    To live its brief moment.

Religions build walls round our love, and science
Is equal of error and truth. Yet always we find
Such ordered purpose in cell and in galaxy,
So great a glory in life-thrust and mind-range,
Such widening frontiers to draw out our longings,
    We grow to one world through
    Enlargement of wonder.

Conflict

When I see the falling bombs
Then I see defended homes.
Men above and men below
Die to save the good they know.

Through the wrong the bullets prove
Shows the bravery of love.
Pro and con have single stem
Half a truth dividing them.

Between the dagger and the breast
The bond is stronger than the beast.
Prison, ghetto, flag and gun
Mark the craving for the One.

Persecution's cruel mouth
Shows a twisted love of truth.
Deeper than the rack and rope
Lies the double human hope.

My good, your good, good we seek
Though we turn no other cheek.
He who slays and he who's slain
Like in purpose, like in pain.

Who shall bend to single plan
The narrow sacrifice of man?
Find the central human urge
To make a thousand roads converge?

Old Song

far voices
and fretting leaves
this music the
hillside gives

but in the deep
Laurentian river
an elemental song
for ever

a quiet calling
of no mind
out of long aeons
when dust was blind
and ice hid sound

only a moving
with no note
granite lips
a stone throat

Caring

Caring is loving, motionless,
An interval of more and less
Between the stress and the distress.

After the present falls the past,
After the festival, the fast.
Always the deepest is the last.

This is the circle we must trace,
Not spiralled outward, but a space
Returning to its starting place.

Centre of all we mourn and bless,
Centre of calm beyond excess,
Who cares for caring, has caress.

Bonne Entente

The advantages of living with two cultures
Strike one at every turn,
Especially when one finds a notice in an office building:
'This elevator will not run on Ascension Day';
Or reads in the *Montreal Star*:
'Tomorrow being the Feast of the Immaculate Conception,
There will be no collection of garbage in the city';
Or sees on the restaurant menu the bilingual dish:

DEEP APPLE PIE
TARTE AUX POMMES PROFONDES

Calamity

A laundry truck
Rolled down the hill
And crashed into my maple tree.
It was a truly North American calamity.
Three cans of beer fell out
(Which in itself was revealing)
And a jumble of skirts and shirts
Spilled onto the ploughed grass.
Dogs barked, and the children
Sprouted like dandelions on my lawn.
Normally we do not speak to one another on this avenue,
But the excitement made us suddenly neighbours.
People exchanged remarks
Who had never been introduced
And for a while we were quite human.
Then the policeman came –
Sedately, for this was Westmount –
And carefully took down all names and numbers.
The towing truck soon followed,
Order was restored.
The starch came raining down.

ROBERT FINCH

b. 1900

Jardin de la Chapelle Expiatoire

Expiatory chapel, chains
Of iron and ivy bind the lanes
Below the lightning-rodded dome
That spikes the sun upon your tomb

Where nurses, children, lovers, fools
And wise, and birds, forget their rôles
Watching time guillotine the heads
Of lilics in the lily beds,

While tears from chestnut candles drop
A wreath of wax, and in the shop
Hard by the marchand de couronnes
Retrieves them in a porcelain one.

Newspapers crackle and hoops roll.
The bench unfurls its slatted scroll
To let a Latin lover's arm
Perturb the Saxon sense of form.

Je t'aimerai toujours! – Toujours? –
Toujours, voilà ce qu'est l'amour.
The obedient clock across the park
Marks time all day to that remark.

Trop radical? Monsieur! Je dis . . .
Peut-êtr' que non, peut-êtr' que oui.
The fate of France goes balancing
With pince-nez on a shaken string.

Faut broder tout autour, serré,
Comm' ça ça fait plus distingué.
The mould of fashion is reset
While Louis romps with Antoinette.

Veux-tu te taire! Viens ici!
M'entends-tu? Tu seras puni!

And shaded by historic woes
A mother mops her infant's nose.

Train Window

The dark green truck on the cement platform
is explicit as a paradigm.
Its wheels are four black cast-iron starfish.
Its body, a massive tray of planking,
ends in two close-set dark green uprights
crossed with three straight cross-pieces, one
looped with a white spiral of hose.

The truck holds eleven cakes of ice,
each cake a different size and shape.
Some look as though a weight had hit them.
One, solid glass, has a core of sugar.
They lean, a transitory Icehenge,
in a moor of imitation snow
from the hatchet's bright wet-sided steel.

Five galvanized pails, mottled, as if
of stiffened frosted caracul, three
with crescent lids and elbowed spouts,
loom in the ice, their half-hoop handles
linking that frozen elocution
to the running chalk-talk of powder-red
box-cars beyond, while our train waits here.

Alone

Carry your grief alone,
No other wants it,
Each man has his own,
A fool flaunts it.

Alone, but not unique:
Bubble to bubble
Is not more like
Than trouble to trouble.

Alone, but light in the end,
For time shall whittle
It like the word of a friend
And the body's fettle.

Alone, to the end, and through
To join the solaced,
The steady journey due
To grief's ballast.

The Statue

A small boy has thrown a stone at a statue,
And a man who threatened has told a policeman so.
Down the pathway they rustle in a row,
The boy, the man, the policeman. If you watch you

Will see the alley of trees join in the chase
And the flower-beds stiffly make after the boy,
The fountains brandish their cudgels in his way
And the sky drop a blue netting in his face.

Only the statue unmoved in its moving stillness
Holds the park as before the deed was done
On a stone axis round which the trio whirls.

Stone that endured the chisel's cutting chillness
Is tolerant of the stone at its foot of stone
And the pigeon sitting awry on its carved curls.

Silverthorn Bush

I am a dispossessed Ontario wood
That took the circling weather as my crown,
Now noise makes havoc of my whispered mood
And enterprise has laughed my towers down.

Is there a poem where I blossom still?
Do paintings keep my solitude secure?
Somewhere remote adventure must distil
Part of its fragrance from an air so pure.

I am the springing memory of my past
In vagabond and child who held me dear,
Theirs is the surest witness that I last
In buds of mine that I no longer bear.

If you can overtake their truant youth
Ask them to flash my secret on your sight,
They heard my pensive river spill its truth
And felt my hidden fibres tug the light.

The riddle is how disappearance puts
A dusty end to a green revery
Yet leaves me nourished by so many roots
That I shall never cease ceasing to be.

A. J. M. SMITH

1902–80

The Lonely Land

Cedar and jagged fir
uplift sharp barbs
against the gray
and cloud-piled sky;
and in the bay
blown spume and windrift
and thin, bitter spray
snap
at the whirling sky;
and the pine trees
lean one way.

A wild duck calls
to her mate,
and the ragged
and passionate tones
stagger and fall,
and recover,
and stagger and fall,
on these stones –
are lost
in the lapping of water
on smooth, flat stones.

This is a beauty
of dissonance,
this resonance
of stony strand,
this smoky cry
curled over a black pine
like a broken
and wind-battered branch
when the wind
bends the tops of the pines

and curdles the sky
from the north.

This is the beauty
of strength
broken by strength
and still strong.

News of the Phoenix

They say the Phoenix is dying, some say dead.
Dead without issue is what one message said,
But that has been suppressed, officially denied.

I think myself the man who sent it lied.
In any case, I'm told, he has been shot,
As a precautionary measure, whether he did or not.

Ode: On the Death of William Butler Yeats

An old thorn tree in a stony place
Where the mountain stream has run dry,
Torn in the black wind under the race
Of the icicle-sharp kaleidoscopic white sky,
  Bursts into sudden flower.

Under the central dome of winter and night
A wild swan spreads his fanatic wing.
Ancestralled energy of blood and power
Beats in his sinewy breast. And now the ravening
Soul, fulfilled, his first-last hour
  Upon him, chooses to exult.

Over the edge of shivering Europe,
Over the chalk front of Kent, over Eire,
Dwarfing the crawling waves' amoral savagery,
Daring the hiding clouds' rhetorical tumult,
  The white swan plummets the mountain top.

The stream has suddenly pushed the papery leaves!
It digs a rustling channel of clear water
On the scarred flank of Ben Bulben.
The twisted tree is incandescent with flowers.

The swan leaps singing into the cold air:
  This is a glory not for an hour:
  Over the Galway shore
  The white bird is flying
  Forever, and crying
  To the tumultuous throng
Of the sky his cold and passionate song.

The Plot against Proteus

This is a theme for muted coronets
To dangle from debilitated heads
Of navigation, kings, or riverbeds
That rot or rise what time the seamew sets
Her course by stars among the smoky tides
Entangled. Old saltencrusted Proteus treads
Once more the watery shore that water weds
While rocking fathom bell rings round and rides.

Now when the blind king of the water thinks
The sharp hail of the salt out of his eyes
To abdicate, run thou, O Prince, and fall
Upon him. This cracked walrus skin that stinks
Of the rank sweat of a mermaid's thighs
Cast off, and nab him; when you have him, call.

The Archer

Bend back thy bow, O Archer, till the string
Is level with thine ear, thy body taut,
Its nature art, thyself thy statue wrought
Of marble blood, thy weapon the poised wing

Of coiled and aquiline Fate. Then, loosening, fling
The hissing arrow like a burning thought
Into the empty sky that smokes as the hot
Shaft plunges to the bullseye's quenching ring.

So for a moment, motionless, serene,
Fixed between time and time, I aim and wait;
Nothing remains for breath now but to waive
His prior claim and let the barb fly clean
Into the heart of what I know and hate –
That central black, the ringed and targeted grave.

Far West

Among the cigarettes and the peppermint creams
Came the flowers of fingers, luxurious and bland,
Incredibly blossoming in the little breast.
And in the Far West
The tremendous cowboys in goatskin pants
Shot up the town of her ignorant wish.

In the gun flash she saw the long light shake
Across the lake, repeating that poem
At Finsbury Park.
But the echo was drowned in the roll of the trams –
Anyway, who would have heard? Not a soul.
Not one noble and toxic like Buffalo Bill.

In the holy name *bang! bang!* the flowers came
With the marvellous touch of fingers
Gentler than the fuzzy goats
Moving up and down up and down as if in ecstasy
As the cowboys rode their skintight stallions
Over the barbarous hills of California.

The Wisdom of Old Jelly Roll

How all men wrongly death to dignify
Conspire, I tell. Parson, poetaster, pimp,
Each acts or acquiesces. They prettify,
Dress up, deodorise, embellish, primp,
And make a show of Nothing. Ah, but met-
aphysics laughs: she touches, tastes, and smells
– Hence knows – the diamond holes that make a net.
Silence resettled testifies to bells.
'Nothing' depends on 'Thing', which is or was:
So death makes life or makes life's worth, a worth
Beyond all highfalutin' woes or shows
To publish and confess. 'Cry at the birth,
Rejoice at the death,' old Jelly Roll said,
Being on whiskey, ragtime, chicken, and the scriptures fed.

The Sorcerer

There is a sorcerer in Lachine
Who for a small fee will put a spell
On my beloved, who has sea-green
Eyes, and on my doting self as well.

He will transform us, if we like, to goldfish:
We shall swim in a crystal bowl,
And the bright water will go swish
Over our naked bodies; we shall have no soul.

In the morning the syrupy sunshine
Will dance on our tails and fins.
I shall have her then all for mine,
And Father Lebeau will hear no more of her sins.

Come along, good sir, change us into goldfish.
I would put away intellect and lust,
Be but a red gleam in a crystal dish,
But kin of the trembling ocean, not of the dust.

R. G. EVERSON

b.1903

Child with Shell

We two lying on sand –
dozens of wrestling lovers twined
in never-ending August love –
while a child scrapes scrapes a shell,
the inside,
to get the deep watery colour off.

Not turned back by Quebec citadel
or mountains pressing down from the land,
the tide
pushes far inland here towards Trois-Rivières.

The child scrapes scrapes away
at the shell –
always the same swirling colour shown;
it won't come off.
A waste of time, child. It's in the bone,
like tides and love.

When I'm Going Well

When I'm going well
as now at Westmount Glen and CPR
in wet October dusk, the winds
taste firecrackery. Loud sparks
jump up laughing like a Breughel bride.
Crayoned in phosphorus, the station agent
vibrates. He's electrocuted.

When I'm electrocuted
weather doesn't matter: wet
dusk of October flashes fire well
like Summer moon, March mud.

I dance on tiptoe mind along the platform
shaking laughter's outstretched hands
that shock me like a Winter lightswitch.

When I'm a Winter lightswitch
I pick allusions off the railway tracks.
Climbing a signal standard, I wave my hat.
A girl walking by along the platform
explodes the whole Glen area.

Rogue Pearunners

We drove – our autoload gang – through the growing season,
a stroll of beaters spread along seed farms,
uprooting rogue pearunners and wild flowers
                    to nourish the chosen seed.

                    I felt religious
in a priest-walk meadow of green-leather peastrings
that held earth down safely. Thousands of acres
in the townships of Rama, Mara and Thora
                    blurred back under my mind.

I am dismayed in anger at rogue pearunners
                    and strange flowering weeds.
I strangle all peculiar growing things,
            hating them worse than abstract artistry.

I suffer an apprehension of petals,
                    lest the mind open
with intuitions and imaginings.

Supermarket

Doors swing open a miracle before me
as I march from the supermarket
my big bass drum of paper bag embraced on pounding lungs
Plumed rhubarb blazes above my head

Men and women with delicious lives
whiz away in autos
through their expanding universe

Some say the universe will round down
into a squeezed testicle
heavier than scale-weight grocer's thumb
screaming louder than tyres from this temporary parking

Widening his mouth grandly
small Jeanot squeezes an orange over his face
joyfully splashing his lifeblood as he goes

I see the glowing earth
stain our sweet boy with brown age-markings

Herd of Stars

The stars are a larger herd than buffalo
and an excellent opportunity
for clubby sportsmen, but we can't kill Heaven
easily as passenger pigeons, baby seals
or the celebrated last Great Auk at Fogo Island.

We could shatter the moon with a rocket
and end our fine days blowing out the sun.
The gun clubs likely can't get many stars
from the herd far off and careless of mankind.

EARLE BIRNEY

b.1904

Pacific Door

Through or over the deathless feud
of the cobra sea and the mongoose wind
you must fare to reach us
Through hiss and throttle come
by a limbo of motion humbled
under cliffs of cloud
and over the shark's blue home.
Across the undulations of this slate
long pain and sweating courage chalked
such names as glimmer yet
Drake's crewmen scribbled here their paradise
and dying Bering lost in fog
turned north to mark us off from Asia still
Here cool Cook traced in sudden blood his final bay
and scurvied traders trailed the wakes of yesterday
until the otter rocks were bare
and all the tribal feathers plucked
Here Spaniards and Vancouver's boatmen scrawled
the problem that is ours and yours
that there is no clear Strait of Anian
to lead us easy back to Europe
that men are isled in ocean or in ice
and only joined by long endeavour to be joined
Come then on the waves of desire that well forever
and think no more than you must
of the simple unhuman truth of this emptiness
that down deep below the lowest pulsing of primal cell
tar-dark and still
lie the bleak and forever capacious tombs of the sea

The Bear on the Delhi Road

Unreal   tall as a myth
by the road the Himalayan bear
is beating the brilliant air
with his crooked arms
About him two men   bare
spindly as locusts   leap

One pulls on a ring
in the great soft nose   His mate
flicks   flicks with a stick
up at the rolling eyes

They have not led him here
down from the fabulous hills
to this bald alien plain
and the clamorous world   to kill
but simply to teach him to dance

They are peaceful both   these spare
men of Kashmir   and the bear
alive is their living   too
If   far on the Delhi way
around him galvanic they dance
it is merely to wear   wear
from his shaggy body the tranced
wish forever to stay
only an ambling bear
four-footed in berries

It is no more joyous for them
in this hot dust to prance
out of reach of the praying claws
sharpened to paw for ants
in the shadows of deodars

It is not easy to free
myth from reality
or rear this fellow up
to lurch   lurch with them
in the tranced dancing of men

Bushed

He invented a rainbow but lightning struck it
shattered it into the lake-lap of a mountain
so big his mind slowed when he looked at it

Yet he built a shack on the shore
learned to roast porcupine belly and
wore the quills on his hatband

At first he was out with the dawn
whether it yellowed bright as wood-columbine
or was only a fuzzed moth in a flannel of storm
But he found the mountain was clearly alive
sent messages whizzing down every hot morning
boomed proclamations at noon and spread out
a white guard of goat
before falling asleep on its feet at sundown

When he tried his eyes on the lake   ospreys
would fall like valkyries
choosing the cut-throat
He took then to waiting
till the night smoke rose from the boil of the sunset

But the moon carved unknown totems
out of the lakeshore
owls in the beardusky woods derided him
moosehorned cedars circled his swamps and tossed
their antlers up to the stars
Then he knew   though the mountain slept   the winds
were shaping its peak to an arrowhead
poised

But by now he could only
bar himself in and wait
for the great flint to come singing into his heart

Slug in Woods

For eyes he waves greentipped
taut horns of slime They dipped
hours back across a reef
a salmonberry leaf
Then strained to grope past fin
of spruce Now eyes suck in
as through the hemlock butts
of his day's ledge there cuts
a vixen chipmunk Stilled
is he – green mucus chilled
or blotched and soapy stone
pinguid in moss alone
Hours on he will resume
his silver scrawl illume
his palimpsest emboss
his diver's line across
that waving green illim-
itable seafloor Slim
young jay his sudden shark
the wrecks he skirts are dark
and fungussed firlogs whom
spirea sprays emplume
encoral Dew his shell
while mounting boles foretell
of isles in dappled air
fathoms above his care
Azygous muted life
himself his viscid wife
foodward he noses cold beneath his sea
So spends a summer's jasper century

EARLE BIRNEY

A Walk in Kyoto

All week   the maid tells me   bowing
her doll's body at my mat   is Boys' Day
Also please Man's Day   and gravely
bends deeper   The magnolia sprig in my alcove
is it male?   The old discretions of Zen were not shaped
for my phallic western eye   There's so much discretion
in this small bowed body of an empire
the wild hair of waterfalls combed straight
in the ricefields   the inn-maid retreating
with the face of a shut flower   I stand hunched
and clueless like a castaway in the shoals of my room

When I slide my parchment door to stalk awkward
through Lilliput gardens framed and untouchable
as watercolors   the streets look much the same
the Men are pulled past on the strings of their engines
the legs of the Boys are revolved by a thousand pedals
and all the faces as taut and unfestive as Moscow's
or Chicago's   or mine

Lord Buddha help us all there is vigor enough
in these islands and in all islands reefed and resounding
with cities   But the pitch is high as the ping
of cicadas   those small strained motors concealed
in the propped pines by the dying river   and only
male as the stretched falsetto of actors mincing
the women's roles in *kabuki*   or female only
as the lost heroes womanized in the Ladies' Opera
Where in these alleys jammed with competing waves
of signs in two tongues and three scripts
can the simple song of a man be heard?

By the shoguns' palace   the Important Cultural Property
stripped for tiptoeing schoolgirls   I stare at the staring
penned carp that flail on each other's backs
to the shrunk pool's edge for the crumb this non-fish
tossed   Is this the Day's one parable?
Or under that peeling pagoda the five hundred tons
of hermaphrodite Word?

At the inn I prepare to surrender again my defeated
shoes to the bending maid   But suddenly the closed
lotus opens to a smile and she points
over my shoulder   above the sagging tiles   to where
tall in the bare sky and huge as Gulliver
a carp is rising   golden and fighting
thrusting its paper body up from the fist
of a small boy on an empty roof   higher
and higher   into the endless winds of the world

El Greco: Espolio

The carpenter is intent on the pressure of his hand

on the awl   and the trick of pinpointing his strength
through the awl to the wood   which is tough
He has no effort to spare for despoilings
or to worry if he'll be cut in on the dice
His skill is vital to the scene   and the safety of the state
Anyone can perform the indignities   It's his hard arms
and craft that hold the eyes of the convict's women
There is the problem of getting the holes exact
(in the middle of this elbowing crowd)
and deep enough to hold the spikes
after they've sunk through those bared feet
and inadequate wrists he knows are waiting behind him

He doesn't sense perhaps that one of the hands
is held in a curious gesture over him –
giving   or asking   forgiveness? –
but he'd scarcely take time to be puzzled by poses
Criminals come in all sorts   as anyone knows who makes
crosses
are as mad or sane as those who decide on their killings
Our one at least has been quiet so far
though they say he has talked himself into this trouble
a carpenter's son who got notions of preaching

Well heres a carpenter's son who'll have carpenter sons,
God willing and build what's wanted temples or tables
mangers or crosses and shape them decently
working alone in that firm and profound abstraction
which blots out the bawling of rag-snatchers
To construct with hands knee-weight braced thigh
keeps the back turned from death

But it's too late now for the other carpenter's boy
to return to this peace before the nails are hammered

Irapuato

For reasons any
                brigadier
                        could tell
this is a favourite nook for
                          massacre
Toltex by Mixtex Mixtex by Aztex
Aztex by Spanishtex Spanishtex by
Mexitex by Mexitex by Mexitex by Texaco

So any farmer can see how the strawberries
are the biggest and reddest
    in the whole damn continent

but why
        when arranged under
                            the market flies

do they look like small clotting hearts?

ALFRED G. BAILEY

b. 1905

Shrouds and Away

The great fear is expected to flash
and curl the toenails of the curly ape,
too self-domesticated yet to scream
and fold his arms up in a sliding down,
his punctured skull as by a forty-five
away in the mesquite, away back
in the atomic saloons of the cowboy frontier,
not alone but replete with buckskin death.
Saddled was no way to escape, as even
Dodge City, or Tombstone, or Bisbee
could grow in a red fester
                    over the chest of the earth
from the heart outwards and into the
                    fronded parts,
leaving them listless, and tested without meaning
or direction or hate. For to fare upwards
in a new life of the heart, keeping the
head turned lifeward, it was essential
to unloop the soul on a mountain peak
and stock up on new (if such could be found)
lodes of a kind of ore we could not assay
                    from prior experience,
(to turn back was certain death in the dark)
but one demanding a naked advance into a
                    land of terror and flowering saguaro
because even the greatest philosophers have
sides that droop and lie about their
loins and mock the lean
and ever-recurrent splendour of the eaglet.

LEO KENNEDY

b. 1907

Words for a Resurrection

Each pale Christ stirring underground
Splits the brown casket of its root,
Wherefrom the rousing soil upthrusts
A narrow, pointed shoot,

And bones long quiet under frost
Rejoice as bells precipitate
The loud, ecstatic sundering,
The hour inviolate.

This Man of April walks again –
Such marvel does the time allow –
With laughter in His blessèd bones,
And lilies on His brow.

Mole Talk

The weasel and the wren consort,
  Beneath one coverlet,
Upon the whittled bones of each
  Docility is set;
Strange fellows for a common bed,
  The rodent and the bird
Lip-deep in sand and gravel, lie
  Without a grudging word.
No shuddering disports the worm,
  Too wise are they, and proud,
To lift a stiffened limb, or pluck
  The seaming of a shroud.

JOHN GLASSCO

1909–1981

Quebec Farmhouse

Admire the face of plastered stone,
The roof descending like a song
Over the washed and anointed walls,
Over the house that hugs the earth
Like a feudal souvenir: oh see
The sweet submissive fortress of itself
That the landscape owns!

And inside is the night, the airless dark
Of the race so conquered it has made
Perpetual conquest of itself,
Upon desertion's ruin piling
The inward desert of surrender,
Drawing in all its powers, puffing its soul,
Raising its arms to God.

This is the closed, enclosing house
That set its flinty face against
The rebel children dowered with speech
To break it open, to make it live
And flower in the cathedral beauty
Of a pure heaven of Canadian blue –
The larks so maimed

They still must hark and hurry back
To the paradisal place of gray,
The clash of keys, the click of beads,
The sisters walking leglessly,
While under the wealth and weight of stone
All the bright demons of forbidden joy
Shriek on, year after year.

Utrillo's World

I

He sat above it, watching it recede,
A world of love resolved to empty spaces,
Streets without figures, figures without faces,
Desolate by choice and negative from need.
But the hoardings weep, the shutters burn and bleed;
Colours of crucifixion, dying graces,
Spatter and cling upon these sorrowful places.
– Where is the loved one? Where do the streets lead?

There is no loved one. Perfect fear
Has cast out love. And the streets go on forever
To blest annihilation, silently ascend
To their own assumption of bright points in air . . .
It is the world that counts, the endless fever,
And suffering that is its own and only end.

II

Anguished these sombre houses, still, resigned.
Suffering has found no better face than wood
For its own portrait: tears are not so good
As the last reticence of being blind.
Grief without voice, mourning without mind,
I find your silence in this neighbourhood;
These hideous places ransom with their blood
The shame and self-loathing of mankind.

They are also masks that misery has put on
Over the faces and the festivals:
Madness and fear must have a place to hide,
And murder a secret room to call its own.
We know they are prisons also, the thin walls
Between us and what cowers and shakes inside.

Brummell at Calais

A foolish useless man who had done nothing
All his life long but keep himself clean,
Locked in the glittering armour of a pose
Made up of impudence, chastity and reserve –
How does his memory still survive his world?

The portraits show us only a tilted nose,
Lips full blown, a cravat and curly wig,
And a pair of posturing eyes,
Infinitely vulnerable, deeply innocent,
Their malice harmless as a child's:

And he has returned to childhood now, his stature
That of the Butterfly whose *Funeral*
He sang (his only song) for one of his
Dear duchesses, Frances or Georgiana,
In the intolerable metre of Tom Moore –

To a childhood of sweet biscuits and curaçao;
Hair-oil and tweezers make him forget his debts,
The angle of his hat remains the same,
His little boots pick their way over the cobblestones,
But where is he going as well as going mad?

Nowhere: his glory is already upon him,
The fading Regency man who will leave behind
More than the ankle-buttoning pantaloon!
For see, even now in the long implacable twilight,
The triumph of his veritable art,

An art of being, nothing but being, the grace
Of perfect self-assertion based on nothing,
As in our vanity's cause against the void
He strikes his elegant blow, the solemn report of those
Who have done nothing and will never die.

One Last Word

For M. McC.

Now that I have your hand, let me persuade you
The means are more important than the end,
Ends being only an excuse for action,
For adventures sought for their own sake alone,
Pictures along the way, feelings
Released in love: so, acting out our dreams
We justify movement by giving it a purpose
(Who can be still forever?)
This is the rationale of travel
And the formula of lovers.

Dearest, it is not for the amusement of certain tissues,
Nor for whatever may thread our loins like a vein
of miraculous water
That now (under the music) I speak your name –
But for the journey we shall take together
Through a transfigured landscape
Of beasts and birds and people
Where everything is new.
Listen,
The embarkation for Cythera
Is eternal because it ends nowhere:
No port for those tasselled sails! And for our love
No outcome,
Only the modesty
The perfection
Of the flight or death of a bird.

A. M. KLEIN

1909–72

Heirloom

My father bequeathed me no wide estates;
No keys and ledgers were my heritage;
Only some holy books with *yahrzeit* dates
Writ mournfully upon a blank front page –

Books of the Baal Shem Tov, and of his wonders;
Pamphlets upon the devil and his crew;
Prayers against road demons, witches, thunders;
And sundry other tomes for a good Jew.

Beautiful: though no pictures on them, save
The scorpion crawling on a printed track;
The Virgin floating on a scriptural wave,
Square letters twinkling in the Zodiac.

The snuff left on this page, now brown and old,
The tallow stains of midnight liturgy –
These are my coat of arms, and these unfold
My noble lineage, my proud ancestry!

And my tears, too, have stained this heirloomed ground,
When reading in these treatises some weird
Miracle, I turned a leaf and found
A white hair fallen from my father's beard.

The Still Small Voice

The candles splutter; and the kettle hums;
The heirloomed clock enumerates the tribes,
Upon the wine-stained table-cloth lie crumbs
Of matzoh whose wide scattering describes
Jews driven in far lands upon this earth.
The kettle hums; the candles splutter; and
Winds whispering from shutters tell re-birth

Of beauty rising in an eastern land,
Of paschal sheep driven in cloudy droves;
Of almond-blossoms colouring the breeze;
Of vineyards upon verdant terraces;
Of golden globes in orient orange-groves.
And those assembled at the table dream
Of small schemes that an April wind doth scheme,
And cry from out the sleep assailing them:
Jerusalem, next year! Next year, Jerusalem!

From *The Psalter of Avram Haktani*

PSALM VI

A psalm of Abraham, concerning that which
he beheld upon the heavenly scarp:

I

And on that day, upon the heavenly scarp,
The hosannahs ceased, the hallelujahs died,
And music trembled on the silenced harp.
An angel, doffing his seraphic pride,
Wept; and his tears so bitter were, and sharp,
That where they fell, the blossoms shrivelled and died.

II

Another with such voice intoned his psalm
It sang forth blasphemy against the Lord.
Oh, that was a very imp in angeldom,
Who, thinking evil, said no evil word –
But only pointed, at each *Te Deum*
Down to the earth, and its abhorrèd horde.

III

The Lord looked down, and saw the cattle-cars:
Men ululating to a frozen land.
He saw a man tear at his flogged scars,

And saw a babe look for its blown-off hand.
Scholars, he saw, sniffing their bottled wars,
And doctors who had geniuses unmanned.

IV

The gentle violinist whose fingers played
Such godly music, washing a pavement, with lye,
He saw. He heard the priest who called His aid.
He heard the agnostic's undirected cry.
Unto Him came the odor Hunger made,
And the odor of blood before it is quite dry.

V

The angel who wept looked into the eyes of God.
The angel who sang ceased pointing to the earth.
A little cherub, now glimpsing God's work flaw'd,
Went mad, and flapped his wings in crazy mirth.
And the good Lord said nothing, but with a nod
Summoned the angels of Sodom down to earth.

PSALM XII

To the chief musician, who played
for the dancers:

These were the ones who thanked their God
With dancing jubilant shins:
The beggar, who for figleaf pride
Sold shoelaces and pins;
The blindman for his brotherly dog;
The cripple for his chair;
The mauled one for the blessed gasp
Of the cone of sweet kind air.
I did not see this dance, but men
Have praised its grace; yet I
Still cannot fathom how they danced,
Or why.

The Rocking Chair

It seconds the crickets of the province. Heard
in the clean lamplit farmhouses of Quebec, –
wooden, – it is no less a national bird;
and rivals, in its cage, the mere stuttering clock.
To its time, the evenings are rolled away;
and in its peace the pensive mother knits
contentment to be worn by her family,
grown-up, but still cradled by the chair in which she sits.

It is also the old man's pet, pair to his pipe,
the two aids of his arithmetic and plans,
plans rocking and puffing into market-shape;
and it is the toddler's game and dangerous dance.
Moved to the verandah, on summer Sundays, it is,
among the hanging plants, the girls, the boy-friends,
sabbatical and clumsy, like the white haloes
dangling above the blue serge suits of the young men.

It has a personality of its own;
is a character (like that old drunk Lacoste,
exhaling amber, and toppling on his pins);
it is alive; individual; and no less
an identity than those about it. And
it is tradition. Centuries have been flicked
from its arcs, alternatively flicked and pinned.
It rolls with the gait of St Malo. It is act

and symbol, symbol of this static folk
which moves in segments, and returns to base, –
a sunken pendulum: *invoke, revoke;*
loosed yon, leashed hither, motion on no space.
O, like some Anjou ballad, all refrain,
which turns about its longing, and seems to move
to make a pleasure out of repeated pain,
its music moves, as if always back to a first love.

Bread

Creation's crust and crumb, breaking of bread,
Seedstaff and wheatwand of all miracles,
By your white fiat, at the feast-times said,
World moves, and is revived the shrouded pulse!
Rising, as daily rises the quickening east,
O kneading of knowledge, leaven of happiness,
History yearns upon your yearning yeast!
No house is home without your wifeliness.

No city stands up from its rock-bound knees
Without your rustic aid. None are elect
Save you be common. All philosophies
Betray them with your yokel dialect.

O black-bread hemisphere, oblong of rye,
Crescent and circle of the seeded bun,
All art is builded on your geometry,
All science explosive from your captured sun.

Bakers most priestly, in your robes of flour,
White Levites at your altar'd ovens, bind,
Bind me forever in your ritual, your
Worship and prayer, me, and all mankind!

MALCOLM LOWRY

1909–57

'Cain shall not slay Abel today on our good ground'

Cain shall not slay Abel today on our good ground,
Nor Adam stagger on our shrouded moon,
Nor Ishmael lie stiff in 28th Street,
With a New Bedford harpoon in his brain,
His right lung in a Hoboken garboon.
For this is the long day when the lost are found,
And those, parted by tragedy, meet
With spring-sweet joy. And those who longest should have met
Are safe in each other's arms not too late.
Today the forsaken one of the fold is brought home,
And the great cold, in the street of the vulture, are warm,
The numbered albatross is sheltered from the storm,
The tortured shall no longer know alarm
For all in wilderness are free from harm:
Age dreaming on youth, youth dreaming on age, shall not be
  found,
While good Loki chases dragons underground.
Life hears our prayer for the lonely trimmer on watch,
Or shuddering, at one bell, on the wet hatch,
At evening, for the floating sailor by the far coast,
The impaled soldier in the shell-hole or the hail,
The crew of the doomed barque sweeping into the sunset
With black sails; for mothers in anguish and unrest
And each of all the oppressed, a compassionate ghost
Will recommend the Pentecost.
Ah, poets of God's mercy, harbingers of the gale,
Now I say the lamb is brought home, and Gogol
Wraps a warm overcoat about him . . .
Our city of dreadful night will blossom into a sea-morning!
Only bear with us, bear with my song,
For at dawn is the reckoning and the last night is long.

Lupus in Fabula

Those animals that follow us in dream,
And mean I know not what! But what of those
That hunt us, snuff, stalk us out in life, close
In upon it, belly-down, haunt our scheme
Of building, with shapes of delirium,
Symbols of death, heraldic, and shadows
Glowering? – Just before we left Tlampam
Our cats lay quivering under the maguey;
A meaning had slunk, and now died, with them.
The boy slung them half stiff down the ravine,
Which now we entered, and whose name is hell.
But still our last night had its animal:
The puppy, in the cabaret, obscene,
Looping-the-loop, and dirtying the floor,
And fastening itself to that horror
Of our last night: and the very last day
While I sat bowed, frozen over mescal,
They dragged two shrieking fawns through the hotel
And slit their throats, behind the barroom door . . .

DOROTHY LIVESAY

b. 1909

Eve

Beside the highway
at the motel door
    it roots
the last survivor of a pioneer
    orchard
miraculously still
    bearing.

A thud another apple falls
    I stoop and O
that scent, gnarled, ciderish
    with sun in it
that woody pulp
    for teeth and tongue
    to bite and curl around
that spurting juice
    earth-sweet!

In fifty seconds, fifty summers sweep
    and shake me –
I am alive! can stand
    up still
hoarding this apple
    in my hand.

The Uninvited

Always a third one's there
where any two are walking out
along a river-bank so mirror-still
sheathed in sheets
of sky pillows of cloud –
their footprints crunch the hardening earth

their eyes delight in trees   stripped clean
winter-prepared
with only the rose-hips red
and the plump fingers of sumach

And always between the two
(scuffing the leaves, laughing
and fingers locked)
goes a third lover   his or hers
who walked this way with one or other   once
flung back the head   snapped branches of dark pine
in armfuls   before snowfall

I walk beside you
trace
a shadow's shade
skating on silver
hear
another voice
singing under ice

Rowan   Red Rowan

All my tears have turned to ice
winter enclosed   crystal
pale mouth   stiff
and the smile   frozen

If I walk in the snow's yard
fir arms laden
a few bright berries storm my eyes
rowan   red rowan

If I pause by a bare tree
snow down shaken
the jewelled jay and the chickadee
are less forsaken

I cannot cry till the far green time
when the hills loosen
and the tears in streams rove through my veins
into frenzied blossom

Waking in the Dark

Whenever I see him
in mind's eye
I see him light-haired and laughing
running in a green field

But day comes
radio is turned on
newspaper is insinuated
under the door
and there   between comic strips
ads   and girdled girls
black words mushroom:

It's going to take a hundred years
            the experts say
to finish this genocide
a hundred years to annihilate a people
to bitter the ricefields with blood
dry Delta's water into salt –
a hundred years
            so our grandchildren growing up
            and their children
will be humans who feel no pity
            for the green earth
and who look upon procreation
            with indifference

When I see my grandchild running
in a game of football
his helmet is empty
in his right arm
he carries his head.

RALPH GUSTAFSON

b. 1909

In the Yukon

In Europe, you can't move without going down into history.
Here, all is a beginning. I saw a salmon jump,
Again and again, against the current,
The timbered hills a background, wooded green
Unpushed through; the salmon jumped, silver.
This was news, was commerce, at the end of the summer
The leap for dying. Moose came down to the water edge
To drink and the salmon turned silver arcs.
At night, the northern lights played, great over country
Without tapestry and coronations, kings crowned
With weights of gold. They were green,
Green hangings and great grandeur, over the north
Going to what no man can hold hard in mind,
The dredge of that gravity, being without experience.

Of Green Steps and Laundry

The man will put a large-headed nail,
Shiny as silver, into the green step,
Straightening winter's bias and spring
Thaw and his hammer will knock it crooked,
The bird come obtrusively to the bough above,
And it will have to be done again, and that
Will be important; and she will hang
Blue and white shirts and a patched quilt
On the laundry line that runs from the kitchen
Step to the yard telephone pole and sheets
That smell of winter's cold, and the pulley
Each time the line is launched will squeak,
And that will be important; and neither
She nor the man pounding the clear air

Fixing the green step with another nail,
Will be aware of the importance, twenty
Years later thought of by him
Who drove nails and saw laundry,
Who thought little of cardinals and clothespins
And now loves life, loves life.

Hyacinths with Brevity

You will use whatever watering can
You can, what knife to plant the bulbs.
I smell leaves and crab-apples
On the ground; the crabbed progression is under
Way, blossom poured, jelly
In jars crimson in the sun along
The sill. That hardens it, you tell me.
I shall have toast in the morning.
        But be quick.
The valves of the heart are pesky things
And shut down. We shall no more see
The like of these leaves again. They blow
Across the garden with this brief wind
That blows. So you will use what you can.
This trowel with last summer's caked
Dirt on the blade, and this can
And these forty bulbs which should be
Already in the ground so swift the wind
Blows and brief the constituency
Of sun. This piece of hose will do . . .
But you have the watering can . . .

A Pile of Grave-Slates

Oh, swept away, swept away,
Death is for all. But death's memorials,

These grave-slates in a heap from what
Skullduggery. Who knows? And what assortment?
What love assignable, what grief,
To each of these, in a broken heap?
The sun shines and East Coker is quiet,
The ashes of Eliot inside, the village
About its church. Sheep crop and time
Is assignable. O these, stones tumbled,
Hunked to the side, lost from their graves,
Put aside, what name for them, ashen
Grey, knocked, O these illegible,
What of these, this elegy, this grey
Accumulation? Enough time,
There is no elegy. In my beginning
Is my end.
Ha.

Hearing the Woodthrush in the Evening

Through the screen-door in the early night,
The song of the thrush. After sundown
He sings. I listen and the wonder is not
Of one song, exactness is about me,
The truth of the world that even as the heart
Responds exactness comes, such as
Music loved and heard again
Provides and love provides, no sooner
We turn from the lake where the moon is
Than the glory of a night without moonlight
Is remembered glorious with fallen stars
Reflected – nothing of our own making
(As being in love, sensitive for the moment,
Or in the compensation of a remorse
Or in the tyranny of other happening)
Grace of itself, renewed,
The short phrase of the nightthrush
All over again we can hardly take it.

There! again. In the falling night –
The tragic song coming through
The kitchen-screen where I stand –
Repeated though I had not asked.

The Philosophy of the Parthenon

Proportion is all things of beauty.
Dimension, go beyond dimension,
Calculation, measure nothing,
Only in relation, the cornice balanced
Against the line, the line against
The truth, not as an existence
But as a meaning, the marble line
The respect to itself, the incumbent gods.

ANNE WILKINSON

1910–61

Lens

I

The poet's daily chore
Is my long duty:
To keep and cherish my good lens
For love and war
And wasps about the lilies
And mutiny within.

My woman's eye is weak
And veiled with milk;
My working eye is muscled
With a curious tension,
Stretched and open
As the eyes of children;
Trusting in its vision
Even should it see
The holy holy spirit gambol
Counterheadwise,
Lithe and warm as any animal.

My woman's iris circles
A blind pupil;
The poet's eye is crystal,
Polished to accept the negative,
The contradictions in a proof
And the accidental
Candour of the shadows;
The shutter, oiled and smooth
Clicks on the grace of heroes
Or on some bestial act
When lit with radiance
The afterwords the actors speak
Give depths to violence,

Or if the bull is great
And the matador
And the sword
Itself the metaphor.

II

In my dark room the years
Lie in solution,
Develop film by film.
Slow at first and dim
Their shadows bite
On the fine white pulp of paper.

An early snap of fire
Licking the arms of air
I hold against the light, compare
The details with a prehistoric view
Of land and sea
And cradles of mud that rocked
The wet and sloth of infancy.

A stripe of tiger, curled
And sleeping on the ribs of reason
Prints as clear
As Eve and Adam, pearled
With sweat, staring at an apple core;
And death, in black and white
Or politic in green and Easter film,
Lands on steely points, a dancer
Disciplined to the foolscap stage,
The property of poets
Who command his robes, expose
His moving likeness on the page.

'In June and gentle oven'

In June and gentle oven
Summer kingdoms simmer
As they come

And flower and leaf and love
Release
Their sweetest juice.

No wind at all
On the wide green world
Where fields go stroll-
ing by
And in and out
An adder of a stream
Parts the daisies
On a small Ontario farm.

And where, in curve of meadow,
Lovers, touching, lie,
A church of grass stands up
And walls them, holy, in.

Fabulous the insects
Stud the air
Or walk on running water,
Klee-drawn saints
And bright as angels are.

Honeysuckle here
Is more than bees can bear
And time turns pale
And stops to catch its breath
And lovers slip their flesh
And light as pollen
Play on treble water
Till bodies reappear
And a shower of sun
To dry their languor.

Then two in one the lovers lie
And peel the skin of summer
With their teeth
And suck its marrow from a kiss
So charged with grace
The tongue, all knowing
Holds the sap of June
Aloof from seasons, flowing.

A Cautionary Tale

. . . we had sold our death . . . for the sum of £70. 18s. 6d. and lent our fear . . . on interest of £3. 10s. 0d. per month, so we did not care about death and we did not fear again.

From *The Palm Wine Drinkard* by Amos Tutuola

She met a lion face to face
As she went walking
Up to her hips in grass
On the wild savannah.
So close they stood they touched
If she put out her thumb
Or he his soft ferocious paw.
She bore no weight of fear,
For only yesterday
She'd leased it to a rich man, poor
In that commodity.
Without her terror she was free
From the alarming smell
That irritates a lion
And makes him lash his tail.
And so he yawned, and stretched
On the long stemmed grasses,
And in the pouring sun
She sat beside his royalty
And sang to him a tale of moon.

Before he rose to go
He opened wide his jaw
And took between his teeth
Her wishing bone, as if to say,
I could, you know.
A rich man had her caution
So she laughed; cool,
In the lion's ear, her pretty breath.
What happened next happens
To every maiden fair
Who lends her fear
But forgets to sell her death:

The lion ate her up, and down
To the smallest crumb.
Lord have mercy upon
Her sweet white bones. Amen.

From *Nature Be Damned*

I took my watch beside the rose;
I saw the worm move in;
And by the tail I yanked him out
And stamped him dead, for who would choose
To leave alive a sin?

The pale rose died of grief. My heel
Had killed its darling foe,
Worm that cuddles in the heart
To ravish it. If worm not tell
How should rose its fairness know?

IRVING LAYTON

b. 1912

The Swimmer

The afternoon foreclosing, see
The swimmer plunges from his raft,
Opening the spray corollas by his act of war –
The snake heads strike
Quickly and are silent.

Emerging see how for a moment
A brown weed with marvellous bulbs,
He lies imminent upon the water
While light and sound come with a sharp passion
From the gonad sea around the Poles
And break in bright cockle-shells about his ears.

He dives, floats, goes under like a thief
Where his blood sings to the tiger shadows
In the scentless greenery that leads him home,
A male salmon down fretted stairways
Through underwater slums . . .

Stunned by the memory of lost gills
He frames gestures of self-absorption
Upon the skull-like beach;
Observes with instigated eyes
The sun that empties itself upon the water,
And the last wave romping in
To throw its boyhood on the marble sand.

Composition in Late Spring

When Love ensnares my mind unbidden
            I am lost in the usual way
On a crowded street or avenue
Where I am lord of all the marquees,

And the traffic cop moving his lips
        Like a poet composing
Whistles a discovery of sparrows
About my head.

My mind, full of goats and pirates
        And simpler than a boy's,
I walk through a forest of white arms
That embrace me like window-shoppers;
Friends praise me like a Turkish delight
        Or a new kind of suspender
And children love me
Like a story.

Conscience more flat than cardboard
        Over the gap in a sole,
I avoid the fanatic whose subway
Collapsed in his brain;
There's a sinking, but the madonna
        Who clings to my hairlock
Is saved: on shore the damned ones
Applaud with the vigour of bees.

The sparrows' golden plummeting
        From fearful rooftop
Shows the flesh dying into sunshine.
Fled to the green suburbs, Death
Lies scared to death under a heap of bones.
        Beauty buds from mire,
And I, a singer in season, observe
Death is a name for beauty not in use.

No one is more happy, none can do more tricks.
        The sun melts like butter
Over my sweetcorn thoughts;
And, at last, both famous and good
I'm a Doge, a dog
        At the end of a terrace
Where poems like angels like flakes of powder
Quaver above my prickling skin.

The Birth of Tragedy

And me happiest when I compose poems.
Love, power, the huzza of battle
are something, are much;
yet a poem includes them like a pool
water and reflection.
In me, nature's divided things –
tree, mould on tree –
have their fruition;
I am their core. Let them swap,
bandy, like a flame swerve
I am their mouth; as a mouth I serve.

And I observe how the sensual moths
big with odour and sunshinc
dart into the perilous shrubbery;
or drop their visiting shadows
upon the garden I one year made
of flowering stone to be a footstool
for the perfect gods:
who, friends to the ascending orders,
will sustain this passionate meditation
and call down pardons
for the insurgent blood.

A quiet madman, never far from tears,
I lie like a slain thing
under the green air the trees
inhabit, or rest upon a chair
towards which the inflammable air
tumbles on many robins' wings;
noting how seasonably
leaf and blossom uncurl
and living things arrange their death,
while someone from afar off
blows birthday candles for the world.

The Fertile Muck

There are brightest apples on those trees
  but until I, fabulist, have spoken
they do not know their significance
or what other legends are hung like garlands
  on their black boughs twisting
like a rumour. The wind's noise is empty.

Nor are the winged insects better off
  though they wear my crafty eyes
wherever they alight. Stay here, my love;
you will see how delicately they deposit
  me on the leaves of elms
or fold me in the orient dust of summer.

And if in August joiners and bricklayers
  are thick as flies around us
building expensive bungalows for those
who do not need them, unless they release
  me roaring from their moth-proofed cupboards
their buyers will have no joy, no ease.

I could extend their rooms for them without cost
  and give them crazy sundials
to tell the time with, but I have noticed
how my irregular footprint horrifies them
  evenings and Sunday afternoons:
they spray for hours to erase its shadow.

How to dominate reality? Love is one way;
  imagination another. Sit here
beside me, sweet; take my hard hand in yours.
We'll mark the butterflies disappearing over the hedge
  with tiny wristwatches on their wings:
our fingers touching the earth, like two Buddhas.

Cain

Taking the air rifle from my son's hand,
I measured back five paces, the Hebrew
In me, narcissist, father of children,
Laid to rest. From there I took aim and fired.
The silent ball hit the frog's back an inch
Below the head. He jumped at the surprise
Of it, suddenly tickled or startled
(He must have thought) and leaped from the wet sand
Into the surrounding brown water. But
The ball had done its mischief. His next spring
Was a miserable flop, the thrust all gone
Out of his legs. He tried – like Bruce – again,
Throwing out his sensitive pianist's
Hands as a dwarf might or a helpless child.
His splash disturbed the quiet pondwater
And one old frog behind his weedy moat
Blinking, looking self-complacently on.
The lin's surface at once became closing
Eyelids and bubbles like notes of music
Liquid, luminous, dropping from the page
White, white-bearded, a rapid crescendo
Of inaudible sounds and a crones' whispering
Backstage among the reeds and bulrushes
As for an expiring Lear or Oedipus.

But Death makes us all look ridiculous.

Consider this frog (dog, hog, what you will)
Sprawling, his absurd corpse rocked by the tides
That his last vain spring had set in movement.
Like a retired oldster, I couldn't help sneer,
Living off the last of his insurance:
Billows – now crumbling – the premiums paid.
Absurd, how absurd. I wanted to kill
At the mockery of it, kill and kill
Again – the self-infatuate frog, dog, hog,
Anything with the stir of life in it,
Seeing the dead leaper, Chaplin-footed,
Rocked and cradled in this afternoon

Of tranquil water, reeds, and blazing sun,
The hole in his back clearly visible
And the torn skin a blob of shadow
Moving when the quiet poolwater moved.
O Egypt, marbled Greece, resplendent Rome,
Did you also finally perish from a small bore
In your back you could not scratch? And would
Your mouths open ghostily, gasping out
Among the murky reeds, the hidden frogs,
We climb with crushed spines toward the heavens?

When the next morning I came the same way
The frog was on his back, one delicate
Hand on his belly, and his white shirt front
Spotless. He looked as if he might have been
A comic; tapdancer apologizing
For a fall, or an Emcee, his wide grin
Coaxing a laugh from us for an aside
Or perhaps a joke we didn't quite hear.

El Cusano

From the place where I was sitting
I watched the weary stone-splitters
Building a road to blot out the sun;
And seeing their sweating bodies
In the merciless, mid-day heat
I wished I could do it for them:
Turn it out like a light, I mean.
And I almost rose up to do so
When my eyes suddenly picked out
A strange, never-before-seen worm
Making its way on the dried leaves.
It had a rich, feudal colour,
Reddish-brown like the Spanish soil
And knew its way among the stones
So plentiful in Alicante.
I love lizards and toads; spiders, too

And all humped and skin-crinkled creatures
But most in love I am with worms.
These sages never ask to know
A man's revenue or profession;
And it's not at antecedents
Or at class that they draw their line
But will dine with impartial relish
On one who splits stones or sells fish
Or, if it comes to that, a prince
Or a generalissimo.
Bless the subversive, crawling dears
Who here are the sole underground
And keep alive in the country
The idea of democracy.
I gave it a mock-Falangist
Salute and it crawled away; or
Was it the stone-splitters frightened
The worm off and the brittle noise
Of almond-pickers? It vanished
Under a dusty dried-up leaf
For a restful snooze in the ground
But I imagine it now tunnelling
Its hard way to Andalusia
Faithful to the colourful soil
Under the villas and motels
Of those whose bankers let them stow
Ancient distinctions and treasure
In the rear of their foreign cars.
O plundered, sold-out, and lovely
Shore of the Mediterranean:
This worm shall knit the scattered plots
Of your traduced, dismembered land;
And co-worker of wave and wind,
Proud, untiring apostle to
The fragrant and enduring dust,
Carry its political news
To Castile and to Aragon.

Early Morning Sounds

Ripe plums are on the table.
I can bang the cupboard door shut.
Eternity dots the kitchen with particulars.

Why should I listen to the impotent whirr
of wings, the buzz-buzz of fat flies,
the sunlight shrunk to what's on their backs?
To a chromatic sneer?

What have I to do with hell's shriekdoms
or the pursy sons of Abraham?
What fly threatens foreclosure
if I don't turn up my hearing-aid?

In my garden the only sounds I hear
are leaves rustling, the receding purr of tires.
The morning glory opens its countenance
to the world. How fresh everything smells.

Remote from all men lie for and kill
I am on holy ground. The innocence
of nature's cannibalism heals and purifies.
The grass's whispering stuns me.

GEORGE JOHNSTON

b. 1913

War on the Periphery

Around the battlements go by
Soldier men against the sky,
Violent lovers, husbands, sons,
Guarding my peaceful life with guns.

My pleasures, how discreet they are!
A little booze, a little car,
Two little children and a wife
Living a small suburban life.

My little children eat my heart;
At seven o'clock we kiss and part,
At seven o'clock we meet again;
They eat my heart and grow to men.

I watch their tenderness with fear
While on the battlements I hear
The violent, obedient ones
Guarding my family with guns.

Music in the Air

What noise up there?
What but a duck in the moon-bright
Neck-sustaining air
Giving a quack to the night?

He makes the sky his pond and drowns the street
And drowns me too, homing on fishy feet
To where my doorway sucks its scaly mouth:
Heaven is north, and my drowned home is south,
And there my caverned coal fire covets me
Of the duck's night. Quack! in the dark, says he.

DOUGLAS LE PAN

b. 1914

Canoe-trip

What of this fabulous country
Now that we have it reduced to a few hot hours
And sun-burn on our backs?
On this south side the countless archipelagoes,
The slipway where titans sent splashing the last great glaciers;
And then up to the foot of the blue pole star
A wilderness,
The pinelands whose limits seem distant as Thule,
The millions of lakes once cached and forgotten,
The clearings enamelled with blueberries, rank silence about them;
And skies that roll all day with cloud-chimeras
To baffle the eye with portents and unwritten myths,
The flames of sunset, the lions of gold and gules.
Into this reservoir we dipped and pulled out lakes and rivers,
We strung them together and made our circuit.
Now what shall be our word as we return,
What word of this curious country?

It is good,
It is a good stock to own though it seldom pays dividends.
There are holes here and there for a gold mine or a hydro-plant.
But the tartan of river and rock spreads undisturbed,
The plaid of a land with little desire to buy or sell.
The dawning light skirls out its independence;
At noon the brazen trumpets slash the air;
Night falls, the gulls scream sharp defiance;
Let whoever comes to tame this land, beware!
Can you put a bit to the lunging wind?
Can you hold wild horses by the hair?
Then have no hope to harness the energy here,
It gallops along the wind away.
But here are crooked nerves made straight,
The fracture cured no doctor could correct.
The hand and mind, reknit, stand whole for work;
The fable proves no cul-de-sac.

Now from the maze we circle back;
The map suggested a wealth of cloudy escapes;
That was a dream, we have converted the dream to act.
And what we now expect is not simplicity,
No steady breeze, or any surprise,
Orchids along the portage, white water, crimson leaves.
Content, we face again the complex task.

And yet the marvels we have seen remain.
We think of the eagles, of the fawns at the river bend,
The storms, the sudden sun, the clouds sheered downwards.
O so to move! With such immaculate decision!
O proudly as waterfalls curling like cumulus!

An Incident

Arrange the scene with only a shade of difference
And he would be a boy in his own native
And fern-fronded providence,
With a map in his hand, searching for a portage overgrown
With brush. Slim he is as a moccasin-flower
With his throat open
To the winds, to the four winds, quivering,
Who alone by the worm-holed flower of the rose-pink house
Bears the weight of this many-ringed, foreign noon,
Shadowless, vast and pitiless.
Notched by the wedge of his frown, it takes no notice.
Light that, alive, would be pungent with resin,
Sapless, now weighs and ponders like limestone.

What is he waiting for
As he studies a map the colour of his youth?
Time stops and whirs in his ear like a humming-bird
As he gazes this way and that
For someone to relieve him
For someone to break through the thicket of his isolation.

In the silence
The grasshoppers crackle and crumble the summer
Between their thin wings
And their singing thighs.
And his head has begun to sing,
To sing with the heat.
Stampeding, his blood butts him like a bull-calf.
How should one so young have learned how to wait?

Ah! there is the relief.
A stray round has caught him at the nape of the neck
And splayed him flat on the earth,
His blood flung wide as a sunburst.

And the pink house, that eavesdropped
Through smoke-blackened holes to each palpitation,
Recovering its reserve,
Sucks in unblemished stillness;
While the wise light with petrified foliage
Having disposed of this awkward animal tremor
Again stands superb as a temple.

The Nimbus

To dive for the nimbus on the sea floor
   Or seek it in the sun
Calls for a plucky steeplejack
   Scaling the sky's giddy ocean
Or dolphin-hearted journeyman
To swim from the foundered sunburst's roar
   With lost treasure on his back.

Ocean that slovens and sidles in vast
   Indifference, hides
In its sludge a wreath of drowning bells.
   Who in those tricky tides
Or up the slippery daybreak's sides
Can grapple the spices of morning fast
   That waste on the listless swells?

Smothered beneath a lowering ceiling
  All cock-crow crispness dies.
Bleary hordes are afraid to wake
  Into the mists that rise
From a palsied swamp where a marsh-bird cries.
Stranger, reconquer the source of feeling
  For an anxious people's sake.

Plunder the mind's aerial cages
  Or the heart's deep catacombs.
O daring's virtuoso, tossed
  Where the furious sunlight foams
Or through the instinct's twilit glooms,
Return with the sunburst's glistering pledges
  As a garland for the lost.

A bittern rusting in the reeds
  Is startled, and through the mist
Whirs screaming. Now, if now only, come
  With the nimbus in your fist.
Strike, strike the rust like a rhapsodist
And burnish gold each throat that pleads
  For dawn's encomium.

R. A. D. FORD

b. 1915

Roadside near Moscow

Bent and heavy with rain,
Staggering in silence, profoundly
Occupied with the secret reconstruction
Of their balance, pine and tamarack
Trees, gathered in profane

Assembly to watch over the slow
Passing of the almost human-like
Column of prisoners, waiting for the snow
To fill in their tracks – strange
Judges of evil done

In many ways. Because I am not
Walking in chains, and am afraid
To look, lest by implication
Glance should be said guilty,
Unhappily turn my head

To the stale spectacle of the sun
Setting among the conifers.
And when it is gone, look down
For the column of men in vain –
In the thick arch of night

That has come suddenly,
Hobble my eyes to perceive
Nothing but the rain, turning
To snow, – all that I wish to see.

Avoiding Greece

Probably it is the rejection
Of the familiar, as if it were
Unnecessary to investigate
What needs no correction,

The mind being drenched
In the sunlight of stones.
Or can we stand perfection
When it is wrenched

From history? I possibly
Prefer like Cavafy
The half perfect of Alexandria.
It is easier passively

To digest, to absorb slowly
Into one's pores. The trouble is
Can one ever be the same
Again, having thus wholly

Tasted of Greece even there
In Africa. Yet still I go
Round the periphery,
Still hesitate to dare

Plunging into the barren
Truth at the dead centre.

Earthquake

The seasons burn. The wind is dry,
Like the tongue of a sickly dog.
The eyes of the fishermen's wives
Are buried in their dark faces
And the children are all armed with knives.

Nothing in the sensuous street gives
Us warning, even cruelty posted
Everywhere, slinking in the shade,
Or unashamed in the meadows
Of cactus that press upon the dead.

Nothing except love – a warning that
Runs before the earthquake to say
That the streets are opening, the fire
Prepared and the waters of the bay
Ready to resume their empire.

It was in the end a small one, the killed
Very few, the fires soon put out. But not
The memory of the woman running above
The blast with her too late warning
And testimony of love.

PATRICK ANDERSON

1915–79

Cold Colloquy

From *Poem on Canada*

What are you . . .? they ask, in wonder.
And she replies in the worst silence of all her woods:
I am Candida with the cane wind.

What are you . . .? they ask again, their mouths full of gum,
their eyes full of the worst silence of the worst winter in a hundred
   years
and the frames of their faces chipped round the skaters' picture –

What are you . . .? they ask.
And she replies: I am the wind that wants a flag.
I am the mirror of your picture
until you make me the marvel of your life.
Yes, I am one and none, pin and pine, snow and slow,
America's attic, an empty room,
a something possible, a chance, a dance
that is not danced. A cold kingdom.

Are you a dominion of them? they ask, scurrying
home on streetcars, skiing the hill's shoulder
and hurrying where the snow is heaping colder and colder.
Are you a dominion of them? they ask.
Most loyal and empirical, she says in ice ironic,
and subject of the king's most gratuitous modesty, she says.
What do you do then?
Lumbering is what I do and whitening is what I wheat,
but I am full of hills and sadness;
snow is where I drift and wave my winds
and as silence my doom, distance is my dream.

Mine are the violet tones of the logs in rivers,
my tallness is the tallness of the pines and the grain elevators
tubular by the scarps of coal, at Quebec.
My caves are the caves of ice but also the holes of Cartier

where the poor squat, numb with winter,
and my poverty is their rags and the prairies' drought.

What is the matter then . . .? they ask, and some are indifferent,
What is the matter then . . .? they ask.

The matter is the sections and the railways, she replies,
and the shouting lost by the way and the train's whistle
like wild-life in the night.
The matter is the promise that was never taken, she replies,
above your heads the cool and giant air
and the future aching round you like an aura –
land of the last town and the distant point,
land of the lumber track losing itself
petering out in the birches, the half-wish
turning back in the wastes of winter or slums
and the skiers lovely and lonely upon the hills
rising in domes of silence. The matter is
the skiers, she replies, athletically lonely,
drowsed in their delight, who hunt and haunt
the centres of their silence and excitement:
finding the cirrus on the high sierras
sluice down the dangers of their dear content –
the matter is being lost in a dream of motion
as larks are in their lights, or bees and flies
glued on the humpbacked honey of summertime.

What should we do then, what should we do . . .? they ask,
out of the factories rattling a new war,
on all the Sundays time has rocked to motion.
What should we do then . . .? they ask, English and French,
Ukrainians, Poles, Finns, at drugstore corners
of streets extended to the ultimate seas
of their defended but ambiguous city.
– Suffer no more the vowels of Canada
to speak of miraculous things with a cleft palate –
let the Canadian,
with glaciers in his hair, straddle the continent,
in full possession of his earth and north
dip down his foot and touch the New York lights
or stir the vegetable matter of the Bahamas

within the Carib gutter. Let
the skiers go with slogans of their eyes
to crowd a country whose near neighbourhood's
the iron kindness of the Russian coasts –
through deserts of snow or dreary wastes of city,
the empty or the emptily crowded North.

And see, she says, the salmon pointing home
from the vast sea, the petalled plethora
and unplumbed darkness of the sea, she says:
gliding along their silvery intuitions
like current on its cables, volt upon volt,
to flash at last, sparking the mountain falls
of Restigouche – spawning a silver million.

P. K. PAGE

b. 1916

The Bands and the Beautiful Children

Band makes a tunnel of the open street
at first, hearing it;
seeing it, band becomes
high; brasses ascending on the strings of sun
build their own auditorium of light,
windows from cornets
and a dome of drums.

And always attendant on bands, the beautiful children,
white with running and innocence;
and the arthritic old
who, patient behind their windows
are no longer split by the quick yellow of imagination
or carried beyond their angular limits of distance.

But the children move
in the trembling building of sound,
sure as a choir
until band breaks and scatters,
crumbles about them and is made of men
tired and grumbling
on the straggling grass.

And the children, lost, lost,
in an open space,
remember the certainty of the anchored home
and cry on the unknown edge of their own city
their lips stiff from an imaginary trumpet.

Element

Feeling my face has the terrible shine of fish
caught and swung on a line under the sun

I am frightened held in the light that people make
and sink in darkness freed and whole again
as fish returned by dream into the stream.

Oh, running water is not rough: ruffled to eye,
to flesh it's flat and smooth; to fish
silken as children's hands in milk.

I am not wishful in this dream of immersion.
Mouth becomes full with darkness
and the shine, mottled and pastel, sounds its own note, not
the fake high treble thrown on resounding faces.

There are flowers – and this is pretty for the summer –
light on the bed of darkness; there are stones
that glisten and grow slime;
winters that question nothing, are a new
night for the passing movement of fine fins;
and quietly, by the reeds or the water fronds
something can cry without discovery.

Ah, in daylight the shine is single
as dime flipped or gull on fire or fish
silently hurt – its mouth alive with metal.

Summer

I grazed the green as I fell
and in my blood
the pigments flowed like sap.
All through my veins the green
made a lacey tree.
Green in my eye grew big as a bell
that gonged and struck
and in a whorl of green in my ear
it spun like a ball.

Orphaned at once that summer
having sprung
full grown and firm with green,
chorussed with fern.

Oh, how the lazy moths were soft upon
my feminine fingers,
how flowers foamed at my knees
all those green months.

Near reeds and rushes where the water lay
fat and lustred by the sun
I sang the green that was in my groin,
the green
of lily and maidenhair and fritillary
from the damp wood
of cedar and cypress from the slow hill,
and the song, stained with the stain of chlorophyll
was sharp as a whistle of grass
in my green blood.

The Stenographers

After the brief bivouac of Sunday,
their eyes, in the forced march of Monday to Saturday,
hoist the white flag, flutter in the snow storm of paper,
haul it down and crack in the midsun of temper.

In the pause between the first draft and the carbon
they glimpse the smooth hours when they were children –
the rise in the ice-cart, the ice-man's name,
the end of the route and the long walk home;

remember the sea where floats at high tide
were sea marrows growing on the scatter-green vine
or spools of grey toffee, or wasps' nests on water;
remember the sand and the leaves of the country.

Bell rings and they go and the voice draws their pencil
like a sled across snow; when its runners are frozen
rope snaps and the voice then is pulling no burden
but runs like a dog on the winter of paper.

Their climates are winter and summer – no wind
for the kites of their hearts – no wind for a flight;
a breeze at the most, to tumble them over
and leave them like rubbish – the boy-friends of blood.

In the inch of the noon as they move they are stagnant.
The terrible calm of the noon is their anguish;
the lip of the counter, the shapes of the straws
like icicles breaking their tongues are invaders.

Their beds are their oceans – salt water of weeping
the waves that they know – the tide before sleep;
and fighting to drown they assemble their sheep
in columns and watch them leap desks for their fences
and stare at them with their own mirror-worn faces.

In the felt of the morning the calico minded,
sufficiently starched, insert papers, hit keys,
efficient and sure as their adding machines;
yet they weep in the vault, they are taut as net curtains
stretched upon frames. In their eyes I have seen
the pin men of madness in marathon trim
race round the track of the stadium pupil.

BERTRAM WARR

1917–43

The Heart to Carry On

Every morning from this home
I go to the aerodrome.
And at evening I return
Save when work is to be done.
Then we share the separate night
Half a continent apart.

Many endure worse than we:
Division means by years and seas.
Home and lover are contained,
Even cursed within their breast.

Leaving you now, with this kiss
May your sleep tonight be blest,
Shielded from the heart's alarms
Until morning I return.
Pray tomorrow I may be
Close, my love, within these arms,
And not lie dead in Germany.

There are Children in the Dusk

Forget the dead, this time
Who are not glorious.
Their sacrifice builds to our crisis,
And the last war left us no sites
To raise our monuments.
We will not weep at unveilings;
Tenderness only confuses
The children who wait in the dusk.

ELDON GRIER

b. 1917

On the Subject of Waves. . .

Mountain teeth, tips of anemious rippled stone,
a glacier of white cloud settled into the tilting passages:

Are you there, Li?

Are you there in the mists, Li Po?

If I ring your two-change name against the massive greys will you
  answer?
On this day and in this location can you see how it is with us
  humans?

There are greens about me here, and the pressure of the soft gloom,
animals in the rising fields.
                    Men I shall never see
stand in the doorways of their huts like true sentinels of life.
There are chimneys behind me rolling up the first balls of pale
  smoke.
A high plateau above, ceaselessly swept with tears of anemia,
before me, and always in my mind is the shape of peninsulas
as insistent as a black mirror.

The empty truck, traumatically still;
A score of men loosely grouped beneath a tree.
                    The stillness is the echo of an explosion!

I find the burlap square in the centre of the road
and I know that beneath it there is a dead child.

Is this what you meant by 'waves', Li Po?

View from a Window

The tenderness so hard to swallow
is partly the two flies settled in her hair.
Her mouth opens to the soothing air,
drools scabs curving down from its edges.

And her brother whom she holds shyly for me to admire . . .
The mess of mucus and the clinging feeding flies . . .
awake, a toxic film covers his eyes
shifting mechanically in patterns of escape.

Across the steeply climbing flat-faced street
at the six vertical ochre strips,
her older sisters, short skirts flaring from the hips,
emerge and blow away buoyant as wasps.

Beauty complicates the average squalor,
carries the unpredictable like fallout
into the brutal levels, burns about
the ruin and the green vine with its yearning.

She hangs around; she says she's eight.
Her name is tuned for ceremonial complaint;
mine is, that dozy flies can travel here without restraint
in the gentlest of hatchures.

In Memory of Garcia Lorca

Garcia Lorca,
Did you think
They'd let it go,
A flower in the lapel
Of perpetual mourning?
Did you guess
The brilliant words
Had made you alien
And (strangely)
Evil?

Granada let you die
Like any freak;
Forgot the day,
Forgot which pit it was.

Gypsies, farmers, generals,
Priests, tourists,
And the quiet rich,
Now pass blandly
Overhead.

Oiga hombre!
Ask around.
Somewhere,
Buried,
Is a silver skull.

Quebec

At steeplecock height
In a tousling wind,
Bands of tourists,
Ants in the spiral
Dimension of birds,
Stalk the pale
Ghosts of history.
Bet on each parroting guide
For signs of the dead.
But brother, nobody's home
Except the river
With its carnival of ships
And the dizzying miles.
Forget your books and cameras.
Dream you flew here
And that lunchtime never comes.
History is in the hotel lounges;
The delicate Wolfe,
Dying in a bed of flags,
Or Montcalm, propped in the backstage
Ruin of battle.

MIRIAM WADDINGTON

b. 1917

The Season's Lovers

In the daisied lap of summer
The lovers lay, they dozed
And lay in sun unending,
They lay in light, they slept
And only stirred
Each one to find the other's lips.
At times they sighed
Or spoke a word
That wavered on uneven breath,
He had no name and she forgot
The ransomed kingdom of her death.

When at last the sun went down
And chilly evening stained the fields,
The lovers rose and rubbed their eyes:
They saw the pale wash of grass
Heighten to metallic green
And spindly tongues of granite mauve
Lick up the milk of afternoon,
They gathered all the scattered light
Of daisies to one place of white,
And ghostly poets lent their speech
To the stillness of the air.
The lovers listened, each to each.

Into the solid wall of night,
The lovers looked, their clearer sight
Went through that dark intensity
To the other side of light.
The lovers stood, it seemed to them
They hung upon the world's rim –
He clung to self, and she to him;
He rocked her with his body's hymn
And murmured to her shuddering cry,
You are all states, all princes I,

And sang against her trembling limbs,
Nothing else is, he sang, *but I.*

They lifted the transparent lid
From world false and world true
And in the space of both they flew.
He found a name, she lost her death,
And summer lulled them in its lap
With leafy lullaby.
There they sleep unending sleep,
The lovers lie
He with a name, she free of death,
In a country hard to find
Unless you read love's double mind
Or invent its polar map.

Thou Didst Say Me

Late as last summer
thou didst say me, love
I choose you, you, only you.
oh the delicate del-
icate serpent of your lips
the golden lie bedazzled
me with wish and flash
of joy and I was fool.

I was fool, bemused
bedazed by summer, still
bewitched and wandering
in murmur hush in green-
ly sketched-in fields
I was, I was, so sweet
I was, so honied with
your gold of love and love
and still again more love.

late as last autumn
thou didst say me, dear,
my doxy, I choose you and
always you, thou didst pledge
me love and through the red-
plumed weeks and soberly
I danced upon your words
and garlanded these
tender dangers.

year curves to ending now
and thou dost say me, wife
I choose another love, and oh
the delicate del-
icate serpent of your mouth
stings deep, and bitter
iron cuts and shapes
my death, I was so fool.

Green World Two

Locked in a glassy iceland lake
I was a child chinning myself
on reflected treetops.
Into my green world
winter shone and splashed
me real with light.

My summer gone,
the knob of light still turns
in that locked lake;
under the seal of ice
the cabined light still burns,
and the yellow haystacks flare
on underwater beaches.
Far above the snow
fills the falling world
to its topmost branches.

Camping

Walking through the unlanterned
darkness, returning to the starcold
glacier of myself after a time
in the hot sun, through the branches looking up
and seeing the stillness
and feeling its edges against my ribs,
I shiver and empty my pocket of stones.

The stones fall to the ground
beside the extinguished fire
and the flap of the tent
rustles in the wind;
yesterday's rain
still falls from the leaves
and I hardly look at the stones.

I look at the dark hollow hole
that waits
patiently for me to return
silent in its knowledge
perfect in its shape
bell-clear in its sound and
unerring in its cold sources
which are my own sources.

MARGARET AVISON

b. 1918

Perspective

A sport, an adventitious sprout
These eyeballs, that have somehow slipped
The mesh of generations since Mantegna?

Yet I declare, your seeing is diseased
That cripples space. The fear has eaten back
Through sockets to the caverns of the brain
  And made of it a sifty habitation.

We stand beholding the one plain
And in your face I see the chastening
Of its small tapering design
That brings up *punkt.*
  (The infinite, you say,
  Is an unthinkable – and pointless too –
  Extension of that *punkt.*)

But ho you miss the impact of that fierce
Raw boulder five miles off? You are not pierced
By that great spear of grass on the horizon?
  You are not smitten with the shock
    Of that great thundering sky?

Your law of optics is a quarrel
Of chickenfeet on paper. Does a train
Run pigeon-toed?

I took a train from here to Ottawa
On tracks that did not meet. We swelled and roared
Mile upon mightier mile, and when we clanged
Into the vasty station we were indeed
Brave company for giants.

Keep your eyes though,
You, and not I, will travel safer back
To Union station.
Your fear has me infected, and my eyes
That were my sport so long, will soon be apt
Like yours to press out dwindling vistas from
The massive flux massive Mantegna knew
And all its sturdy everlasting foregrounds.

Hid Life

Red apples hang frozen
in a stick-dry, snow-dusty
network of branches,
against lamb's wool and pastelblue of sky,
a crooked woodenness, a wizzening red.

Are these iron stems? or is
this tree in a lee out of the
clattering winds?

Heavily in my heart
the frost-bruised fruit, the sombre tree,
this unvisited room off winter's endless corridors
weigh down.

But
even this fruit's flesh
will sodden down at last.

Botanist, does the seed
so long up held
still somehow inform
petal and apple-spring-perfume
for sure, from so far?

Is the weight only
a waiting?

Tennis

Service is joy, to see or swing. Allow
All tumult to subside. Then tensest winds
Buffet, brace, viol and sweeping bow.

Courts are for love and volley. No one minds
The cruel ellipse of service and return,
Dancing white galliardes at tape or net
Till point, on the wire's tip, or the long burn-
ing arc to nethercourt marks game and set.
Purpose apart, perched like an umpire, dozes,
Dreams golden balls whirring through indigo.
Clay blurs the whitewash but day still encloses
The albinos, bonded in their flick and flow.
Playing in musicked gravity, the pair
Score liquid Euclids in foolscaps of air.

Janitor Working on Threshold

Boot-soles and overalled haunches to the street,
kneeling –
bowed from the ivy-falling, darkly-bright
day-ceiling,
and from cool stone, green court inside –
prising some broken stripping loose, and all in
slow skill, plain sight,
working, till no one need be afraid of falling –

this street
and door in the final stilling
of all (of the one at the threshold with the rest)
recall the less than the least,
John, and the wings, and healing.

For Dr and Mrs Dresser

Your doctor, Lord,
from West Irian,
brought pictures of a leaf that served as plate,
and grubs, fat, silkily hirsute, that men
need there for nourishment.
Whoever speak your word
along that coast must share
that feast of fatness first
for love of you and them
who offer from your provenance their best.
The gorge that finds your natural good
in food that squirms is
given aptitude, surely, by grace . . .

As that doctor, Lord,
learned to subsist, in order
to love first-hand, for you, and tell
how God, to His plain table
invites them too, and will
dwell among them who offer Him their all,
You, once for all,
offered and dwelt – you, fairest beyond call
                    of mortal imagining:
here, taking on yourself not only
our spoiled flesh, but the lonely
rot of the rebel, of the solitary,
of all not-God on earth, for all
who claim, in all your range of time. And still
without one queasy tremor, you could wholly
swallow our death, take on our
lumpish wingless being, darkened out
to cold and night – except for
the timeless love
even for us, my Lord.

And having suffered us to glut
the pure well-spring, and having
plumbed even hell, for us, you could
come back, in flesh, living, and
open out the shaft and sweep
of clarity and scope,
flooding us with your risen radiance,
can bid us, in turn, o gentle Saviour:
'take, eat –
live'.

. . . *Person, or A Hymn on and to the Holy Ghost*

How should I find speech
to you, the self-effacing
whose other self was seen
alone by the only one,

to you whose self-knowing
is perfect, known to him,
seeing him only, loving
with him, yourself unseen?

Let the one you show me
ask you, for me,
you, all but lost in
the one in three,

to lead *my* self, effaced
in the known Light,
to be in him released
from facelessness,

so that where you
(unseen, unguessed, liable
to grievous hurt) would go
I may show him visible.

LOUIS DUDEK

b. 1918

The Jungle

Time has its ends and its beginnings –
  leaf-end and stems, skin and liver –
through which the rhythm passes,
  a drum-beat in a jungle silence,
somewhere in the trees the shriek
  of a wild bird shattered by claws,
somewhere the big cats mating, crying
  in pain, possibly in delight,
and the silence is endless, listening to the drums
  day after day with a new beginning,
day after day anguish, possibly pleasure,
  but beyond that the perfect white of the sky
waiting above the world for the movement to cease,
  to be absorbed in the folds of its sea,
to be drowned in space where all that was
  is sound in a deaf ear, fear in a forgotten dream.

The Pomegranate

The jewelled mine of the pomegranate, whose hexagons of honey
The mouth would soon devour but the eyes eat like a poem,
Lay hidden long in its hide, a diamond of dark cells
Nourished by tiny streams which crystallized into gems.

The seeds, nescient of the world outside, or of passionate teeth,
Prepared their passage into light and air, while tender roots
And branches dreaming in the cell-walled hearts of plants
Made silent motions such as recreate both men and fruits.

There, in a place of no light, shone that reddest blood,
And without a word of order, marshalled those grenadiers:
Gleaming without a sun – what art where no eyes were! –
Till broken by my hand, this palace of unbroken tears.

To wedding bells and horns howling down an alley,
Muffled, the married pair in closed caravan ride;
And then, the woman grown in secret, shining white,
Unclothed, mouth to mouth he holds his naked bride.

And there are days, golden days, when the world starts to life,
When streets in the sun, boys, and battlefields of cars,
The colours on a banister, the vendors' slanting stands
Send the pulse pounding on like the bursting of meteors –

As now, the fruit glistens with a mighty grin,
Conquers the room; and, though in ruin, to its death
Laughs at the light that wounds it, wonderfully red,
So that its awful beauty stops the greedy breath.

And can this fact be made, so big, of the body, then?
And is beauty bounded all in its impatient mesh?
The movement of the stars is that, and all their light
Secretly bathed the world, that now flows out of flesh.

From *Europe*

31

The ignorant present has scribbled over the past
                    at Winchester;
an American goon
painted on the door
          saying 'yak yak' to all this
rectangular, proud English Gothic.

At first there was nothing, the beginning
was hardest, then what they made
          was made out of what they had begun.

No matter. The present is shaped out of the first
          shaped stones,
               from Stonehenge to this.

They have written their initials
          beside the dead. New Englishmen

and Americans, make goons
on golden doors.

It is all flowers within
and fluted stems,
'Music,' you said, and 'One cannot believe,'
I said,
'That it is of stone,' such intricate
articulations
of white bone, and terrible black
medieval magic.

But there is nothing,
nothing in the 19th century additions.
The recent
cemetery sculpture looks silly
beside the older, somber, Norman Gothic
that did not even try to be beautiful.
Only true.
To what? Consider for instance
the harrowing tomb of Richard Fox
showing his body
lacerated by suffering and death,
there to tell you
– do not be too gay, even if God
doesn't particularly matter,
the bones remain, they are the cathedral.

But several tourists
have scrawled their names
on the breast of Richard Fox
just where the skeleton comes through the skin.
Let these additions remain
in Winchester
Perhaps time will prove
such fools, like sculptured animals
belong here after all.
They would have had no stone
to write so plainly on, if death had not offered them
its bony breast.

95

The sea retains such images
      in her ever-unchanging waves;
for all her infinite variety, and the forms,
inexhaustible, of her loves,
she is constant always in beauty,
            which to us need be nothing more
      than a harmony with the wave on which we move.
All ugliness is a distortion
of the lovely lines and curves
      which sincerity makes out of hands
            and bodies moving in air.
Beauty is ordered in nature
      as the wind and sea
shape each other for pleasure, as the just
know, who learn of happiness
      from the report of their own actions.

Dawn

I woke up with morning yawning in my mouth
with laughter overflowing a tea-kettle spout;
I woke up with apples rolling in my belly
in a barn, and six thousand fireflies going south.

I had just left a sun from whose milk-white aura
shining in speckled sacraments on teacup and floor
the black wings of the dawn-fly roared like dreams
and fought with two suns on a pin, changing colour:

giving its light to Day, today and many days!
The timeless bug out of a light that never fades
flew out and fluttered like a monkey clapping hands,
and it stood still, so beautiful it left me crazed.

Mouths

Pendulous mouth, you flap in a wind
            on a space-washed skull,
make a wilderness of sound
        brlaa
            brlaa frloo

flapping mouths
        on wind-swept heads –
until two cross to close the gap
between all art and artery, heart and the empty world

        lubb lubbu luvbl
            aluvu

close each other with a skill or will
under that spell
to loose themselves into each other,
            then turn to lose themselves
in that greater mouth
        nothing can still or fill.

ALFRED PURDY

b. 1918

Wilderness Gothic

Across Roblin Lake, two shores away,
they are sheathing the church spire
with new metal. Someone hangs in the sky
over there from a piece of rope,
hammering and fitting God's belly-scratcher,
working his way up along the spire
until there's nothing left to nail on –
Perhaps the workman's faith reaches beyond:
touches intangibles, wrestles with Jacob,
replacing rotten timber with pine thews,
pounds hard in the great cave of the sky,
contends heroically with difficult problems
of gravity, sky navigation and mythopoeia,
his volunteer time and labour donated to God,
minus sick benefits of course on a non-union job –

Fields around are yellowing into harvest,
nestling and fingerling are sky and water borne,
death is yodeling quiet in green woodlots,
and bodies of three young birds have disappeared
in the sub-surface of the new country highway –

That picture is incomplete, part left out
that might alter the whole Dürer landscape:
gothic ancestors peer from medieval sky,
dour faces trapped in photograph albums escaping
to clop down iron roads with matched greys:
work-sodden wives groping inside their flesh
for what keeps moving and changing and flashing
beyond and past the long frozen Victorian day.
A sign of fire and brimstone? A two-headed calf
born in the barn last night? A sharp female agony?
An age and a faith moving into transition,
the dinner cold and new-baked bread a failure,

deep woods shiver and water drops hang pendant,
double yolked eggs and the house creaks a little –
Something is about to happen. Leaves are still.
Two shores away, a man hammering in the sky.
Perhaps he will fall.

The Sculptors

Going thru cases and cases
of Eskimo sculpture
returned from Frobisher
because they said it wasn't
good enough for sale
to T. Eaton Co. Ltd.
Getting itchy excelsior packing
inside my shirt and searching
for one good carving
one piece that says 'I AM'
to keep a southern promise
One 6-inch walrus (tusk broken)
cribbage board (ivory inlay gone)
dog that has to be labeled dog
polar bear (only three bear paws)
what might be a seal (minus flipper)
and I'm getting tired of this
looking for something
not knowing what it is
But I guess they got tired too
looking for rabbit or bear
with blisters from carving tools
dime-sized and inflating
into quarters on their fingers
waiting
for walrus or white whale
under the ice floes to
flop alive on their lap
with twitching faces unready
to taste the shoe blacking

carvers use
for stone polish
I'm a little ashamed of myself
for being impatient with them
but there must be something
there must be something
one piece that glows
one slap-happy idiot seal
alien to the whole seal nation
one anthropomorphic walrus
singing Hallelujah I'm a bum
in a whiskey baritone
but they're all flawed
broken
            bent
                    misshapen
failed animals
with vital parts missing
And I have a sudden vision
of the carvers themselves
in this broken sculpture
as if the time & the place & me
had clicked into brief alignment
and a switch pulled
so that I can see and feel
what it was like to be them
the tb out-patients
failed hunters
who make a noise at the wrong time
or think of something else
at the trigger moment
and shine their eyes
into a continual tomorrow
the losers and failures
who never do anything right
and never will
the unlucky ones
always on the verge
of a tremendous discovery
who finally fail to deceive

even themselves as time begins
to hover around them
the old the old the old
who carve in their own image
of maimed animals
and I'd like to buy every damn case
– *at Pangnirtung.*

Lament for the Dorsets

(*Eskimos extinct in the 14th century* A.D.)

Animal bones and some mossy tent rings
scrapers and spearheads   carved ivory swans
all that remains of the Dorset giants
who drove the Vikings back to their long ships
talked to spirits of earth and water
– a picture of terrifying old men
so large they broke the backs of bears
so small they lurk behind bone rafters
in the brain of modern hunters
among good thoughts and warm things
and come out at night
to spit on the stars

The big men with clever fingers
who had no dogs and hauled their sleds
over the frozen northern oceans
awkward giants
                    killers of seal
they couldn't compete with little men
who came from the west with dogs
Or else in a warm climatic cycle
the seals went back to cold waters
and the puzzled Dorsets scratched their heads
with hairy thumbs around 1350 A.D.
– couldn't figure it out
went around saying to each other
plaintively

'What's wrong? What happened?
Where are the seals gone?'

And died

Twentieth century people
apartment dwellers
executives of neon death
warmakers with things that explode
– they have never imagined us in their future
how could we imagine them in the past
squatting among the moving glaciers
six hundred years ago
with glowing lamps?
As remote or nearly
as the trilobites and swamps
when coal became
or the last great reptile hissed
at a mammal the size of a mouse
that squeaked and fled

Did they ever realize at all
what was happening to them?
Some old hunter with one lame leg
a bear had chewed
sitting in a caribou-skin tent
– the last Dorset?
Let's say his name was Kudluk
and watch him sitting there
carving 2-inch ivory swans
for a dead grand-daughter
taking them out of his mind
the places in his mind
where pictures are
He selects a sharp stone tool
to gouge a parallel pattern of lines
on both sides of the swan
holding it with his left hand
bearing down and transmitting
his body's weight
from brain to arm and right hand

and one of his thoughts
turns to ivory
The carving is laid aside
in beginning darkness
at the end of hunger
and after a while wind
blows down the tent and snow
begins to cover him
After 600 years
the ivory thought
is still warm

The Country North of Belleville

Bush land scrub land –
          Cashel Township and Wollaston
Elzevir McClure and Dungannon
green lands of Weslemkoon Lake
where a man might have some
          opinion of what beauty
is and none deny him
                              for miles –

Yet this is the country of defeat
where Sisyphus rolls a big stone
year after year up the ancient hills
picnicking glaciers have left strewn
with centuries' rubble
                              backbreaking days
                              in the sun and rain
when realization seeps slow in the mind
without grandeur or self deception in
                              noble struggle
of being a fool –

A country of quiescence and still distance
a lean land
          not like the fat south

with inches of black soil on
earth's round belly –
And where the farms are
it's as if a man stuck
both thumbs in the stony earth and pulled

it apart
to make room
enough between the trees
for a wife
and maybe some cows and
room for some
of the more easily kept illusions –
And where the farms have gone back
to forest
are only soft outlines
shadowy differences –

Old fences drift vaguely among the trees
a pile of moss-covered stones
gathered for some ghost purpose
has lost meaning under the meaningless sky
– they are like cities under water
and the undulating green waves of time
are laid on them –

This is the country of our defeat
and yet
during the fall plowing a man
might stop and stand in a brown valley of the furrows
and shade his eyes to watch for the same
red patch mixed with gold
that appears on the same
spot in the hills
year after year
and grow old
plowing and plowing a ten-acre field until
the convolutions run parallel with his own brain –

And this is a country where the young
leave quickly

unwilling to know what their fathers know
or think the words their mothers do not say –

Herschel Monteagle and Faraday
lakeland rockland and hill country
a little adjacent to where the world is
a little north of where the cities are and
sometime
we may go back there
                                        to the country of our defeat
Wollaston Elzevir and Dungannon
and Weslemkoon lake land
where the high townships of Cashel
                                        McClure and Marmora once were –
But it's been a long time since
and we must enquire the way
                    of strangers –

Necropsy of Love

If it came about you died
it might be said I loved you:
love is an absolute as death is,
and neither bears false witness to the other –
But you remain alive.

No, I do not love you
                    hate the word,
that private tyranny inside a public sound,
your freedom's yours and not my own:
but hold my separate madness like a sword,
and plunge it in your body all night long.

If death shall strip our bones of all but bones,
then here's the flesh, and flesh that's drunken-sweet
as wine cups in deceptive lunar light:
reach up your hand and turn the moonlight off,
and maybe it was never there at all,
so never promise anything to me:

but reach across the darkness with your hand,
reach across the distance of tonight,
and touch the moving moment once again
before you fall asleep –

The Blue City

Of such an intense azure
that it seeps into your bones
providing dull earth
with an upsidedown sky
My wife is still sleeping
tired from the long journey
I have awakened very early
and must let her sleep longer
Her face is turned to one wall
of the strange hotel room
not feeling my own excitement
at being here with blood thrumming
and pulse beating a little faster
from the sheer romance of Asia
She turns over and sighs
while I'm standing at the window
trying to glimpse a camel
outside on awakening streets:
a woman is sweeping cobblestones
with some kind of twig broom
charcoal burning in a brazier
much blue ceramic but no camels
It occurs to me that I will remember
this time for its inbetweenness
removed from the continuity of things
and it's as if I'm a long way off
somewhere else and watching myself
watching a woman in bed sleeping
seeing what I see for the second time
the wished-for camel and burning charcoal
a blue city slowly coming awake

the little pulse in my wife's throat
I will be seeing it a second time
or has that second time arrived?
– My wife awakening not exactly
here nor there and aware of oddness
disoriented she keeps looking at me
brown eyes puzzled for a long moment

Samarcand & Ameliasburg

RAYMOND SOUSTER

b. 1921

Eight Pears

Placed there
in the big picture-window
to catch the morning
and afternoon sun,

eight yellow-green
slightly rotund &
very solemn pears

continue to be stubborn
stay hard

fearing our greedy
two sets of teeth
eager to pierce their skins
dig deep into heavenly juices.

Eight pears
sit there in that window

hating the sun
& fighting time
that ripens everything.

The Six-Quart Basket

The six-quart basket
one side gone
half the handle torn off

sits in the centre of the lawn
and slowly fills up
with the white fruits of the snow.

Where the Blue Horses

The street is quiet,
the noise through the wall is stilled,
the little cat curled up on the chair,
radio turned off, milk bottles outside the door.

And for now
nothing but sleep and dreams and thoughts of sleep,
not even love keep us awake tonight

as we sink into that strange land
where the blue horses toss
riderless and proud.

On the Edge

Walking this street going west
into the setting sun I'm locked
so tight in my own thoughts I'm hardly aware
of someone coming toward me:
                                                    then the glare
of the sun suddenly blinds – I only know
a headless man has passed by,
his coat open like a loose cloak
around him –
                        No, I don't turn around
to see if he's old or young, stranger, whatever,
something tells me not to –
                                                and walk on
with the sun slipping over the edge
of my world and me not sure at all
if what passed me was headless
or two-headed, friend or foe:
                                                and if this street
this sun – even this world – is real or unreal . . .

Flight of the Roller Coaster

Once more around should do it, the man confided . . .

and sure enough, when the roller-coaster reached the peak
of the giant curve above me, screech of its wheels
almost drowned out by the shriller cries of the riders,

instead of the dip and plunge with its landslide of screams,
it rose in the air like a movieland magic carpet, some wonderful
bird,

and without fuss or fanfare swooped slowly across the amusement
park,
over Spook's Castle, ice-cream booths, shooting-gallery. And losing
no height

made the last yards above the beach, where the cucumber-cool
brakeman in the last seat saluted
a lady about to change from her bathing-suit.

Then, as many witnesses reported, headed leisurely out over the
water,
disappearing all too soon behind a low-flying flight of clouds.

ELI MANDEL

b. 1922

David

all day the gopher-killing boys
    their sling-shot arms
        their gopher-cries

the king insisting
    my poetry must stop

I have written nothing since May

instead
      walk among the boys
gopher-blood on their stretched
hands
    murder will end murder
the saying goes, someone must
do something about the rodents
and poems do not:
                    even the doctors
    admit that it's plague
    ask me about my arms
                            look
    at my shadow hanging
        like a slingshot

the world turns like a murderous stone
    my forehead aching with stars

Phaeton

The giant wink in a clown's cheek
Shrinks the flared noon of his eye
And then it opens, moony and alarmed,
And spins concentric circles

Like a cartoon of stunned cat
Eye-struck by perpetual brickbats.

The snuff and puff of lung stuff
Wreathes the bright neck, the flashing mane,
The wide nostrils of a painted horse.

I saw this on a parchment once,
Eye, horse, and windy cheek,
Or sat that horse as frightened boy
And felt the sun go round and round
And take me with him by the ten taut reins
Of my skinned and burning hands.

The Madwomen of the Plaza de Mayo

They wear white scarves and shawls.
They carry pictures on strings about their necks.
I have seen their faces elsewhere:
in Ericeira, fishermen's wives
walking in dark processions
to the sea, its roaring,
women of Ireland
wearing their dark scarves
hearing the echo of guns, bombs

Identities
the *desaparecidos*
lost ones
the disappeared

in the Plaza the Presidential Palace
reveals soldiers like fences with steel spikes
the rhythm of lost bodies
the rhythm of loss

A soldier is a man who is not a man.
A fence, a spike
A nail in somebody's eye.
Lost man.

Why are the women weeping?
For whom do they cry
under the orange moon
under the lemon moon of Buenos Aires?

'If only for humanitarian reasons
tell the families of the living
where are they
tell the families of the dead
what they need
what they deserve to know.'

No one speaks.
The junta says nothing.
The *desaparecidos* remain silent.
The moon has no language.

The Moon in All Her Phases

I'd say, in the old manner:
she imagines our existence,
its changes, illusions

well, luminous times are gone
most of my friends quarrel
drink
          are not, though satyrs,
lordly
          recently one in rage
told me he loved the first war
because they sang such songs

we grope toward each other
hands fumble among clothes

I cant remember:
                              did your eyes
your body glow?
                              I can't remember
the difficult lovely words.

ELIZABETH BREWSTER

b. 1922

Where I Come From

People are made of places. They carry with them
hints of jungles or mountains, a tropic grace
or the cool eyes of sea-gazers. Atmosphere of cities
how different drops from them, like the smell of smog
or the almost-not-smell of tulips in the spring,
nature tidily plotted in little squares
with a fountain in the centre; museum smell,
art also tidily plotted with a guidebook;
or the smell of work, glue factories maybe,
chromium-plated offices; smell of subways
crowded at rush hours.

Where I come from, people
carry woods in their minds, acres of pine woods;
blueberry patches in the burned-out bush;
wooden farmhouses, old, in need of paint,
with yards where hens and chickens circle about,
clucking aimlessly; battered schoolhouses
behind which violets grow. Spring and winter
are the mind's chief seasons: ice and the breaking of ice.

A door in the mind blows open, and there blows
a frosty wind from fields of snow.

Romance

Mary tells me she admires the salmon
because it is such a romantic fish.
It travels two thousand miles in order to spawn,
then dies in a ritual of love and death,
its flesh feeding new generations.

But I am relieved to discover
that only Pacific salmon

are in fact so feeble.
Atlantic salmon make the trip to spawn
several times,
though every spawning
leaves another scar
and they are ringed like trees.

There is Time

to begin again
to write new poems for the new land
to start life over
to find a new lover
or a dozen lovers
to follow where the hands beckon
to create
and uncreate.

I am not young
but neither am I old.
I have twenty years
more maybe
before earth takes me
breaks me again
and makes me snail or flower.

'Death is inevitable,'
my old lover said.
'Giving in isn't.'
And I believe
though perhaps he did not believe
himself.

All I have done
seems sometimes waste
scribble on sand
but always
it can be done over.

Not permanence
not the eternal footprints in the sands of
etcetera
but the feel of
writing in sand with a broken stick
rough bark under the fingers
or the feel of toes in wet sand

There is time
yet
I can start again

there is time

MILTON ACORN

b. 1923

Knowing I Live in a Dark Age

Knowing I live in a dark age before history,
I watch my wallet and
am less struck by gunfights in the avenues
than by the newsie with his dirty pink chapped face
calling a shabby poet back for his change.

The crows mobbing the blinking, sun-stupid owl;
wolves eating a hamstrung calf hindend first,
keeping their meat alive and fresh . . . these
are marks of foresight, beginnings of wit:
but Jesus wearing thorns and sunstroke
beating his life and death into words
to break the rods and blunt the axes of Rome;
this and like things followed.

Knowing that in this advertising rainbow
I live like a trapeze artist with a headache,
my poems are no aspirins . . . they show
pale bayonets of grass waving thin on dunes;
the paralytic and his lyric secrets;
my friend Al, union builder and cynic,
hesitating to believe his own delicate poems
lest he believe in something better than himself:
and history, which is yet to begin,
will exceed this, exalt this
as a poem erases and rewrites its poet.

Old Property

Past that frost-cracked rock step
twist yourself through
skewjee trunks and old coat-hook branches;
ground once dug and thought of and
never intended for those toadstools.

In the shade past the crashed robins nest
past that spilt sunlight see
his grainy grip clenched
on a hatchet keened to a leaf,
a man in murky denims
whispering curses to the leaves.

Whale Poem

Sunglare and sea pale as tears.
One long hour we watched the black whales
circling like dancers,
sliding dark backs out of water,
waving their heaved tails,
about an eyepupil-round spot
just a knife-edge
this side of the horizon.

Black whales, let me join in your dance
uncumbered by ego, my soul well anchored
in a brain bigger than I am
. . . multiplied tons of muscled flesh
roaring in organized tones of thunder
for kilometres When I love
let me love gigantically; and when I dance
let the earth take note
as the sea takes note of you.

ROBIN SKELTON

b. 1925

Goat

I have a name for it.
I smell rank
to nostrils of morality.
I thrust home
however shrill the bleat.
My eye is red,
my hairy tangle
knotted stiff with balm.

I know my end.
Exuberant with seed,
I mount the universal
pulse, whose heat
offends your niceties,
and makes you fear
the blinding energies
of lunge and rut,

and use me as an emblem
of the rogue,
the fool, the outlaw,
and, extolled by flame
on midnight moorlands,
the forbidden god
of naked sorceries,
those ancient dreams

I do not have to dream.
No tether can
efface the name I sign
on field and yard;
circling the centre,
I possess my need,
and, ribald, eat
the rubbish of the world

to feed the fury
that the world proclaims,
derides, disguises, cheats:
I am that thing
shame hides and halters
till it bursts its bonds,
and in your farmyards
dance upon my string.

Eagle

Vertigo is my territory. Man
only another movement, another shift
in the arrangement of shadows beneath my shadow,
angular, thick-boned, cumbersome, and bad meat.

I do not trouble him or the larger kind,
having no love of eating on the ground;
I kill what I can bring into my height,
what I can raise up until, terror-stunned,

they watch the dwindling of their day, perceive
the small earth small, self-cancelling, and share
the shock that is the last discovery; here
they learn abandonment of every word

and are self-rent before I rend and eat
what they already have forgotten, locked
on fear and splendour. Image me as God.
I am the final judgement and the rock.

Wart Hog

Moon-tusked, wrenching at roots,
I dream of women.

Once there were sacred boars
in the sacred wood,

eaters of corpses,
guardians of the groves

under the wand of the goddess.
Now I grub,

trample, and squeal,
bulk-shouldered, warted, haired

rank as the sweat of terror,
sour as shame,

guardian of no ritual
but the thrust

through darkness
of the bald horn of the moon.

JAMES REANEY

b. 1926

The Katzenjammer Kids

With porcupine locks
And faces which, when
More closely examined,
Are composed of measle-pink specks,
These two dwarf imps,
The Katzenjammer Kids,
Flitter through their Desert Island world.
Sometimes they get so out of hand
That a blue Captain
With stiff whiskers of black wicker
And an orange Inspector
With a black telescope
Pursue them to spank them
All through that land
Where cannibals cut out of brown paper
In cardboard jungles feast and caper,
Where the sea's sharp waves continually
Waver against the shore faithfully
And the yellow sun above is thin and flat
With a collar of black spikes and spines
To tell the innocent childish heart that
It shines
And warms (see where she stands and stammers)
The dear fat mother of the Katzenjammers.
Oh, for years and years she has stood
At the window and kept fairly good
Guard over the fat pies that she bakes
For her two children, those dancing heartaches.
Oh, the blue skies of that funny paper weather!
The distant birds like two eyebrows close together!
And the rustling paper roar
Of the waves
Against the paper sands of the paper shore!

The Chough

The chough, said a dictionary
Is a relation of the raven
And a relative of the crow.
It's nearly extinct,
But lingers yet
In the forests about Oporto.
So read I as a little child
And saw a young Chough in its nest,
Its very yellow beak already tasting
The delicious eyes
Of missionaries and dead soldiers;
Its wicked mind already thinking
Of how it would line its frowsy nest
With the gold fillings of dead men's teeth.
When I grew older I learned
That the chough, the raven and the crow
That rise like a key signature of black sharps
In the staves and music of a scarlet sunset
Are not to be feared so much
As that carrion bird, within the brain,
Whose name is Devouring Years,
Who gobbles up and rends
All odds and ends
Of memory, good thoughts and recollections
That one has stored up between one's ears
And whose feet come out round either eye.

The Oracular Portcullis

Illyria's hair fell down
Like a long golden answer
To a question in long division.
Gradually she let her saucer down
Crushing the invisible column
Of time and space beneath
Into a gently wounded saucer

And slowly the white portcullis rose,
The cruel ivory portcullis of her mouth
That had closed on both victims and visitors:
Many poached eggs and pieces of toast,
Duchess of Oldenburg apples,
And oceans of broth and soup.
Slowly Illyria made
Her delirious epigram:
'It is surely a well-known fact,
My dear,
That women are concave,
And men are convex?'
Thus spake Illyria; this question she posed,
Then quite quickly her portcullis closed.

The Drunken Preacher's Sermon

From *A Suit of Nettles*
(September Eclogue)

Lo, it was the last supper, I leader from gutter
Tell you tall and short tinkery folks gathered.
What did those white souls eat while their Lord talked:
I don't know indeed I don't, maybe sandwiches.
And He said haughtily head up to the twelve,
'I'll ask you assafoetidae again I will,
Isn't there one, one disciple with the spunk to betray me?'
They all fumbled their food, fed themselves slowly.
'Otherwise you see all my work ought in value is.'
'I will,' quavered weakly woefully poor Judas,
Runty little redhaired man runaway parents from him.
'I'll go through with ghoulish Holy Ghost necessary job.'
Even then at the end of it elder tree saw he.
His death, his Lord's death held at Lord's supper.
So you've all certainly betrayed him so you've done
Something for him by my bottle faith fiddle de dee you have.

MARYA FIAMENGO

b. 1926

For Osip Mandelstam

A 'proletariat of petals and bullets',
presses against my chest.
Breathing is difficult.
I am cold.
I cannot live in such a small
corner of the flesh.
The radar of defeat
like the star of David
glints on my wrist.

(Can you comfort me
Pablo Neruda
for Osip Emilyevich Mandelstam,
a bag of brittle Jewish bones
broken in Siberia.)

The white bleached snow
of Vorkuta
eats at my eyes.
And you impeccable Michael Sholokoff
lend me your Cossacks' rose coloured
sun glasses
because I am blinded by
a collective necessity
which would intern the sun.

Remorseless, implacable destiny
where pogroms fall through the air
like programmes at a Sunday concert,
I would give up everything
especially history
for mercy and justice,
a little tender sanity.

If at the end of the pain,
the blessing;

and clear in the midnight frost
above the walls of the Kremlin
sparkles the dark standard
of the Virgin of Kazan;
even a sulphur match might
keep me warm and alive.

The High Cost of Eternity

Eternity was in our lips and eyes,
but you must have misunderstood
the message
and raced home to mortality.

I understand you live underground
in a crystal palace
surrounded by quartz and stalagmites.
That also is one kind of durability.

But the message spoke of eternity,
and I think bliss was mentioned
and heaven but not home.

Home is where one pays the bills.
Faces debts and debtors.
Heaven is all arrears,
the amplitude of living beyond one's means.

But then not all of us
are given to immortal longings.
And the cost of losing Empires
of any kind
is always high.

ROBERT KROETSCH

b. 1927

There is a World

good morning, monday   you don't
look so hot yourself   you one-eyed
bastard   here in the hard west

we hold each other's bodies/   here
in the coyote night   we howl
the dawn   is just another

dawn/   don't look so self-important
I know she left: I heard the car
too, the quick gravel: it was

a short summer   those three nights
god, I was drunk somewhere   somewhere
we argued   against mortality, made love;

nobody warned us   there is a world
I hear it   the blackbird dawn
flocking the day loud and   hullabaloo

the slow stenographers   caw
the epitaph: I miss you/
what can I add: my bed, hollow

the ring   the coop of heaven
hangs on a hollow sky   a hawk:
I/wishing you here   hold me

free/   my cock's crow to the
rising predator   the scalding day:
there is a world/   I miss you

Anthem

Better the caught coin
than the flung.

O gold have mercy.

Better the last man off
the ship than not at all.

O guts have mercy.

Better married than to bum.

O gonads have mercy.

Better to drink no hemlock
and to manufacture cannons for
the prevention of disease only.

O guns, O guns have mercy.

PHYLLIS WEBB

b. 1927

The Days of the Unicorns

I remember when the unicorns
roved in herds through the meadow
behind the cabin, and how they would
lately pause, tilting their jewelled
horns to the falling sun as we shared
the tensions of private property
and the need to be alone.

Or as we walked along the beach
a solitary delicate beast
might follow on his soft paws
until we turned and spoke the words
to console him.

It seemed they were always near
ready to show their eyes and stare
us down, standing in their creamy
skins, pink tongues out
for our benevolence.

As if they knew that always beyond
and beyond the ladies were weaving them
into their spider looms.

I knew where they slept
and how the grass was bent
by their own wilderness
and I pitied them.

It was only yesterday, or seems
like only yesterday when we could
touch and turn and they came
perfectly real into our fictions.
But they moved on with the courtly sun
grazing peacefully beyond the story
horns lowering and lifting and
lowering.

I know this is scarcely credible now
as we cabin ourselves in cold
and the motions of panic
and our cells destroy each other
performing music and extinction
and the great dreams pass on
to the common good.

Ezra Pound

And among the divine paranoids old Ezra
paces his cage unattached to the mode of doubt
replete with salvation he is 60 years old
under the Pisan sunfire. He sees straight
through the bars into the court of Confucius
then slumps in a corner wondering what went
wrong. His old man's hair is matted with rain
and wardust. His brain is in fever.
Nevertheless he hikes from pole to pole
to plot once more the stars of his fixed
obsession. It seems so clear. If only
they'd listened. They shine light all night
on the perplexity of his predicament.
He stares back, can't sleep, understands
nothing. Jew-hater. Poet. Intellectual.
A curious animal, a-typical, it reads and
writes, shaking and sweating, being so shut in,
the canto arising:
    '*And if the corn be beaten*
    Demeter has lain in my furrow'
the mode of doubt imprisoned for ever and ever
in the style of its own luxury.

DON COLES

b.1928

Nostalgie de Bonheur

'J'ai appris qu'on est plus
malheureux dans le malheur
que dans le bonheur.'
Armand Salacrou

Having been down myself more than I like
Even if so far never quite out,
And finding no shortcuts to up

Just having to sweat it through,
And usually losing weeks
In the process,

Noticing to my soul's chagrin
That at such times even the
Truly superior wisdom

Of favourite authors is no help,
Neither are my own notebooks,
Jottings recording

Against just such need
The endured loneliness
Of admired men,

Passages of real sustenance and
Understanding when encountered in
Less baleful hours,

It now seems time to admit that
Nothing is so much to be avoided
As unhappiness,

A perhaps obvious remark
Except that I have not always
Found it obvious,

Imagining that essential discoveries
Were to be made down there,
A received idea, no doubt,

From a youthful and boring
Source, certainly one only
Marginally borne out

In my own life,
Which has had enough of it now,
Enough time lost in the dark service

And desires now to announce
A late switch,
There is nothing precocious

About me,
From now on I'm for happiness,
At least it's a

Well-documented ambition,
My new slogan is
Down with *Weltschmerz*,

The moon is more beautiful
Through the strayed curtains
Of a man who knows this much

Than it is over all Asia
I'll see how it turns out.

Visit to the Gericare Centre

From *Landslides*

VI

Here are the concentrated moments,
Like landslides, blocking forgetfulness.
Your uncle driving the cart
Into an abandoned barn
In a rainstorm,

Sitting beside him under
The drumming roof, the wind
Leading great paths of rain
Across the roof. Those
Floods of sound

Overhead, the two of you solemn there,
Brimming with noise. Your
Scared, eager enduring.
In a pause, the horse
Shaking its harness.

IX

There is now no pleasure like
The pleasure of being alive then,
On that winter's day you skated
Out along the Châteauguay
Beyond the rim of houses

Towards Aunt Sarah's, or I,
Enough years on,
Sped on the neighbour's rink
Under the blue bulb swinging
At early dusk on its cord,

The ice sown with dazzle
Like a Flemish pond, like
Cuyp's old silvering winters
Below some dormant town.
How cold and clear

It shone, only the
Secret-keeping child could tell –
To skate again that day,
Joy would burst
Our hearts!

XI

When a breath of early freshness
Blows over you, even now
When a breath of a kind of

Fullness re-opens the hiding place
Behind the leaves –

When he parted them
To find you hiding there,
Even now when your young father
Parts the leaves,
Always his face

Bending close towards
Thrilled laughter –
What kings, what legends!
Who is here now to find you
As you were,

Who is here to find you before
The roamings into womanhood,
To find you among the leaves?
Press my hand if you know.
Press it anyway.

XIII

Remembering that line praising 'A mind
In full possession of its experience',
And thinking of you, of all that
Chaos is repossessing behind the
Widening, night-glittering moat,

Sometimes I'll rant, or grieve,
But rather now would sidestep
Eternitywards and glimpse a sort of
Comfort there, out under the stars
Where every man's

In soul-motion,
And know the private life's
Motley and generous
And in its manifoldness flies
Finally above pity,

Its soon-surrendered experience
Full of destructible small glories

Like wings glinting
In odd places under the eaves,
Possessed only as

Rain over a barn's roof is possessed,
As a book shelters a mind
In its brief strength or
A thrilled child laughs even while
Leaves resume their pause,

Shading pressed grass,
All soon restored to time, things
Not important enough for saving,
Images it was sufficient to reflect on
Only a little,

The briefest glance
Towards which may, however,
Deliver us.

D. G. JONES

b. 1929

Northern Water Thrush

The bird walks by the shore
untouched by the falling sun
which crashes in the alders.

Lilting on delicate feet
among the dry reeds, the washed
and broken skeletons of trees,

he moves through his broken world
as one, alone surviving, moves
through the rubble of a recent war:

a world of silence but for the sound
of water tapping on the stones,
a drag of wind in the pine.

Grey with his yellow, fluted breast
he dips and halts, a string of notes
limned on the stillness of a void:

the stillness of the early spring
when new suns prepare
like new buds in the leafless air

a pristine world, the old
calligraphy of living things
having been destroyed.

But though he walks magnificent
upon the littered shore, holding
the moment with his poise,

he too will whiten with the days,
and the flawed human world
return with his delicate bone.

Tremor

Thunder in the earth, today
in Guatemala, the first
quivering of the floor
                                        crocks
tiles falling

heaven reversed, and one goes staggering
into its silence

chicken feathers, dust
and the family effects settle
with the earth's plates

while here in Quebec the snow
drifts and the pit
of an avocado splits

in a glass jar

Thunder, I ask? clearing a space
among the daily papers

One should have ears in his feet
one should read the still air
like a beast

like a seismograph
searching the silence

Even so, up, down
it is there
                in the stove
in the furnace of the stars
in the lungs
                the thunder
shaking the heart

There is No Place

There is no place in this garden
for a 707 or any
aluminum wing

only the first flight of leaves

tracers of bees, caterpillars, small
reddish moths

and the rain

no place for gods, the fission
or fusion of Zeus

Promethean fire
would make matchwood of the picket fence
weathering grey

half a bird's egg is sufficient
proof of violence

sleek stepping stones, no flood

like earth
this remnant of an orchard's vulnerable
to heavenly waste

the airways leak

yet a body might grow quiet in
this modest space

it's not the end of the war
but the raids are seasonal, include
some heavy robins, spring's

green flak

Annunciation

Snow has come back to make of weeds
A window-shopper's garden, frail
Easter Flowers for unbelievers.

But the sun is not the same, nor the hills.
And the silence when I stop the car
Is not the same, is a silence made

For a few birds, their thin
Aerial music. This is the coin
Flung against the brazen tower.

It is the confidence within (not
Of what endures) of what will be.
Distant. It transforms

This window to a world. Again.
The air is not just air, it is an arctic
Confidence of flowers.

JAY MACPHERSON

b. 1931

The Swan

White-habited, the mystic Swan
Walks her rank cloister as the night draws down,
In sweet communion with her sister shade,
Matchless and unassayed.

The tower of ivory sways,
Gaze bends to mirrored gaze:
This perfect arc embraces all her days.
And when she comes to die,
The treasures of her silence patent lie:
'I am all that is and was and shall be,
My garment may no man put by.'

The Day-Labourer

Time is a labourer on God's farm,
And keeps His living things from harm.
He sees the fledglings on the bough
And wards the serpent from their nest;
He leads the Unicorn to plow,
At evening brings him home to rest:
The eternal Phoenix on his arm
Roosts, rustling the warm feathers of her breast.

The Fisherman

The world was first a private park
Until the angel, after dark,
Scattered afar to wests and easts
The lovers and the friendly beasts.

And later still a home-made boat
Contained Creation set afloat,
No rift nor leak that might betray
The creatures to a hostile day.

But now beside the midnight lake
One single fisher sits awake
And casts and fights and hauls to land
A myriad forms upon the sand.

Old Adam on the naming-day
Blessed each and let it slip away:
The fisher of the fallen mind
Sees no occasion to be kind,

But on his catch proceeds to sup;
Then bends, and at one slurp sucks up
The lake and all that therein is
To slake that hungry gut of his,

Then whistling makes for home and bed
As the last morning breaks in red;
But God the Lord with patient grin
Lets down his hook and hoicks him in.

ALDEN NOWLAN

1933–83

The Execution

On the night of the execution
a man at the door
mistook me for the coroner.
'Press,' I said.

But he didn't understand. He led me
into the wrong room
where the sheriff greeted me:
'You're late, Padre.'

'You're wrong,' I told him. 'I'm Press.'
'Yes, of course, Reverend Press.'
We went down a stairway.

'Ah, Mr Ellis,' said the Deputy.
'Press!' I shouted. But he shoved me
through a black curtain.
The lights were so bright
I couldn't see the faces
of the men sitting
opposite. But, thank God, I thought
they can see me!

'Look!' I cried. 'Look at my face!
Doesn't anybody know me?'

Then a hood covered my head.
'Don't make it harder for us,' the hangman whispered.

The Bull Moose

Down from the purple mist of trees on the mountain,
lurching through forests of white spruce and cedar,
stumbling through tamarack swamps,
came the bull moose
to be stopped at last by a pole-fenced pasture.

Too tired to turn or, perhaps, aware
there was no place left to go, he stood with the cattle.
They, scenting the musk of death, seeing his great head
like the ritual mask of a blood god, moved to the other end
of the field, and waited.

The neighbours heard of it, and by afternoon
cars lined the road. The children teased him
with alder switches and he gazed at them
like an old, tolerant collie. The women asked
if he could have escaped from a Fair.

The oldest man in the parish remembered seeing
a gelded moose yoked with an ox for plowing.
The young men snickered and tried to pour beer
down his throat, while their girl friends took their pictures.

And the bull moose let them stroke his tick-ravaged flanks,
let them pry open his jaws with bottles, let a giggling girl
plant a little purple cap
of thistles on his head.

When the wardens came, everyone agreed it was a shame
to shoot anything so shaggy and cuddlesome.
He looked like the kind of pet
women put to bed with their sons.

So they held their fire. But just as the sun dropped in the river
the bull moose gathered his strength
like a scaffolded king, straightened and lifted his horns
so that even the wardens backed away as they raised their rifles.
When he roared, people ran to their cars. All the young men
leaned on their automobile horns as he toppled.

A Tiger in the Dublin Zoo

Know that I am Napoleon, the great, the magnificent tiger.
Observe how an emperor
takes possession of the ground
on which he stands, imposes his own order
on the space around him.
                I walk to and fro,
                and am never halted.
I stop and turn where I choose.
                        And that
is three feet short
of the end of the cage.
                No more and no less.
Never once have I forgotten myself
    and been stopped by the bars.
I am Napoleon, the great, the magnificent tiger.

God Sour the Milk of the Knacking Wench

God sour the milk of the knacking wench
with razor and twine she comes
to stanchion our blond and bucking bull,
pluck out his lovely plumbs.

God shiver the prunes on her bark of chest,
who capons the prancing young.
Let maggots befoul her alive in bed,
and dibble thorns in her tongue.

Plot for a science fiction novel

Scientists from another galaxy
capture an earthling
and decide after examining him
that he is a machine designed
for the manufacture
of shit.

JOE ROSENBLATT

b. 1933

All Worlds Lead to the Lobe

Spirit, I want it to happen:
every morning is bright & early
& crocuses are popping insomniacs
nudging the tempo of summer.

In the garden of moments
the holes walk off a golf course
over to where the sunlight stirs a toadstool
& white rabbits run into the tunnels of tomorrow.

The robin who left his memory down south
returns to the seeded ground to hunt the cheated worm,
the smallest sentinel in my world hops
to the vibrations of love, oblivious of hunger.

Time signals, & bullfrog people leap
into sweating ponds seasoned with flies
circumferences of splashes, widening kingdoms
for the torrid days creeping into the brain bud.

The oceanographer of the inevitable collects
the drops of blue laughter, the nerves of dreams
wind around the incandescent body of the chief voyeur
& grasshoppers of my senses are slaves of ecstasy . . .

Reflections bounce off the billiard table
solipsist spheres roll into the pockets of ears
& little people in boots of metaphor await the thunders
before the minnows of happiness change into adults.

The Spider

In his crocheted embassy
the spinning butler
entertains the lady flies –
monster of his operetta, he
feeds upon a half digested bumblebee.

The spinning butler
feels the guide wires of his planet –
vibrations will send him scampering
on eight allegro fingers:
mealtime is anytime – there's
no refrigerator in that sky.

Fish

I touched the flesh with my eyes.
It was that of a woman with scales.
The lips were thick and closed.
It had swallowed all my symbols.

The phantom appeared and winked.
I kept hauling it up.
The eyes were bluer than mine.
She floundered on the sand
and the sea gleamed.

I pitched my wishes back into the black water.

LEONARD COHEN

b. 1934

Credo

A cloud of grasshoppers
rose from where we loved
and passed before the sun.
I wondered what farms
they would devour,
what slave people would go free
because of them.
I thought of pyramids overturned,
of Pharaoh hanging by the feet,
his body smeared –
Then my love drew me down
to conclude what I had begun.

Later, clusters of fern apart,
we lay.
A cloud of grasshoppers
passed between us and the moon,
going the other way,
each one fat and flying slow,
not hungry for the leaves and ferns
we rested on below.
The smell that burning cities give
was in the air.

Batallions of the wretched,
wild with holy promises,
soon passed our sleeping place;
they ran among
the ferns and grass.
I had two thoughts:
to leave my love
and join their wandering,
join their holiness;
or take my love
to the city they had fled:

That impoverished world
of boil-afflicted flesh
and rotting fields
could not tempt us from each other.

Our ordinary morning lust
claimed my body first
and made me sane.
I must not betray
the small oasis where we lie,
though only for a time.
It is good to live between
a ruined house of bondage
and a holy promised land.
A cloud of grasshoppers
will turn another Pharaoh upside-down;
slaves will build cathedrals
for other slaves to burn.
It is good to hear
the larvae rumbling underground,
good to learn
the feet of fierce or humble priests
trample out the green.

What I'm Doing Here

I do not know if the world has lied
I have lied
I do not know if the world has conspired against love
I have conspired against love
The atmosphere of torture is no comfort
I have tortured
Even without the mushroom cloud
still I would have hated
Listen
I would have done the same things
even if there were no death
I will not be held like a drunkard

under the cold tap of facts
I refuse the universal alibi

Like an empty telephone booth passed at night
and remembered
like mirrors in a movie palace lobby consulted
only on the way out
like a nymphomaniac who binds a thousand
into strange brotherhood
I wait
for each one of you to confess

Another Night with Telescope

Come back to me
    brutal empty room
Thin Byzantine face
    preside over this new fast
I am broken with easy grace
Let me be neither
    father nor child
but one who spins
on an eternal unimportant loom
  patterns of wars and grass
which do not last the night
    I know the stars
are wild as dust
and wait for no man's discipline
    but as they wheel
from sky to sky they rake
  our lives with pins of light

GEORGE BOWERING

b. 1935

Circus Maximus

They come
                    each one
of them
          a rise
like those
                  who came
before them.

New heroes flexing
to fill the shape
made out for them
by the now dead

but each new man
a refutation of his predecessor.

Camus refining Dostoyevsky
yet feeling the swell
of body the Russian felt

the old man
grizzling in his beard
anticipating the African
who would fit his fingers
over the old pen
playing with down
    on his cheek.

Who knows ten of your molecules
are not in me?

but Nature helps me define
my own shape
looks on as
I stumble over the centuries'
exposed root
lost in my own
                          particularity

(patterns I deny
and that
is part of a pattern).

Styles do not multiply themselves
but are all
pervasive

the suit of clothes
is nothing
without its own disfigurations.

New heroes flex into it
and bend it to their bodies.

Winter's Dregs

Thomas Hardy in the stars
a constellation looking down
look around
                    There is Taurus
there is the big bear
there is all the canopy
of eating & killing creatures

crowding all your greek-ending
girls
      And here are we
blast-beruffled more than ever
was robin or nightingale

though now we muffle our souls
our very darkling selves ourselves

In the Elevator

In the elevator
everyone is resentful
of everyone
else's stop.

As if,
dreaming, we
could choose
our various fates.

Silent door
slowly opening sideways
with glimpses of floors
not ours, not ours.

Everyone in the box
knows where
he's going,

he only looks
at the others
when the elevator stops
between floors.

Against Description

I went to the blackberries
on the vine.

They were blackberries
on the vine.

They were
blackberries.

Black
berries.

GEORGE JONAS

b. 1935

Two poems from *The Happy Hungry Man*

Makes a brief political statement the next morning

I wish to be quite accurate.

This Imperial City is not dear to me:
I am not entertained by her circuses
Not impressed by her legions
And I do not adore
Her murderous immaculate gods.

The fire that is now visible
Even after sunrise
As it leaps from one suburban rooftop to the next
Does not take me by surprise
I will not need time
To gather my possessions
I have little desire to escape
And nowhere to escape to.

Some seem to take pleasure
In fanning the flames
And some think it right to do so
But I am not inclined to join them
Fires require no assistance.

Nor will I carry water for in all good conscience
I no more wish to see this city preserved than
destroyed
City of slaves
City of gladiators
City of vestal virgins:
As all roads led to you for quite some time
For quite some time all roads will lead past you.

But unlike many
I have also been outside the gates
Marching with the armies of the barbarians
Exchanging love with them in their own language

And sleeping with my eyes open in their camps
And I am afraid.

I hereby give notice of my intention
To play my fiddle while Rome is burning.

Changes his mind and dials the number again

We are slowly coming of age.
Time does the only thing it can for us in passing.
We'd have to look at some fixed object to notice
It passes at the same speed as we do
Only much faster.

But there are no objects outside of ourselves.
We learn our lessons wrinkle by wrinkle,
Humbly planting behind us now and then
The milestone of a missing tooth.

Forgive me my sister in sequence!
We are water, time is our glass,
It would not serve us to be spilled.

I, for one, will allow it to carry me
To whosoever's lips, until I'm drained.

PAT LOWTHER

1935–75

The Complicated Airflow

The complicated airflow in the house
stirred by my passing sets
the doors to opening and closing
one and then another
in an unknown order
like a pack of cards playing
its own solitaire.
The echoes fade like wooden etudes.
I think sometimes my passage
through this hall is like a falling
down a clef into the sea
and where I hit, a hissing
fault springs on the surface
(warp in a spider web,
spidering of a mirror

What is whiter than hurt water?
What is more flawed than a broken
stave of sound?

Diviners

Are we this – diviners,
Under our gray pearl
Smoke smeared
Sky,
Diviners of sun?

Look –
Where our hands join,
Water,
Green growth,
A townful of new babies,
A season of wine.

GEORGE AMABILE

b. 1936

Prairie

a light word
filled with wistful spokes
of sun through the overcast at dusk
or smoke totems bent at the top
wisping away into beige emulsions

an earth word
a moist darkness turning
stones and roots
fossils and tiny lives
up to the sun

a watery word
mirage and heat lightning
steadied by pewter barns
where whole towns float in a lilting haze
and rumors of rain rise from the rapeseed lakes

a flame shaped word
a ragged mane blowing
for miles across dry grass
lighting the night like fired breath
out of the old testament

a word with air
in its belly that howls
for hours or days and dries
the memory of soft conversation
to wheatdust under the tongue

like the distance we've come
to stand here in the sky at the top of the world

Railroad Switching Yard

These tracks cohabit
in prosperous darkness
like silver eels
over which the diesels
ease their one-eyed hulls and stunted thunders
till the cars jolt and lock
or shudder and scrape free
exchanging origins for destinations.

Shunted on sidings
hauled across town through stopped traffic
left in the rain for days
the boxcars, coalcars, gondolas, tankers
and sometimes a bright caboose
remind us that horizons are not fixed.

They wear insignia like veterans
of our ancient war with space
and bring to our windows and backyard gates
contagious distances
in the names of towns whose legendary ways
died into history
before the engineers
in their puffed hats and coveralls
had learned to roll their first Bull Durham.

LIONEL KEARNS

b. 1937

In-Group

No one
ran up
and shook
Christ's hand.

The only others
with that kind
of inclination

Had theirs
nailed down
too.

Insight

Christ wow
now I get
your message

It's a warning
incarnate, Man –

How this love-junk
can really
get a hold of you

How it can
hang you up
for good

Captivity

How falling snow takes a town at night
in its muffle, takes you, too
standing there under the street light
alone watching giant shadows silently
crash down. And you stay there so long
your ears pick up the tiny tinkle-tink-tink
above you of snowflakes breaking
on the metal lamp-shade. Squeak-slap
squeak-slap squeak-slap someone
in galoshes walks by then fades utterly
into the thickness of whiteness
of darkness. Snowflakes falling
on your face, melting in your eyes
filling your footprints with stillness
Two streets away a truck with loose chains
clanks rhythmically into soft oblivion

International Incident

I was drinking the American's beer
and talking loud and saying things
that seemed unpleasantly true
I was drinking the American's beer
and shouting we should legislate against
foreign take-overs and U.S. control
of colleges, media, land, us
I was drinking the American's beer
and telling him it was all his fault
yes I was drinking the American's beer
and reminding him that it sure takes guts
to be so hostile to your host, but he
thought I was talking about myself

TOM MARSHALL

b. 1938

Astrology

It's an approach. Say what you like
about it. It's an approach.
Speak of the transience of philosophies;
all are de-commissioned at last.
I admit this. It's entirely the point.

I care more about this
arrangement of words than about you.
To return one needs an approach,
'a way of happening',
and any approach will do
in a sense. The one that works
is true (of course, all are true).

Why not then take the intricate
fire of stars as way? Interlocking roses
of our summer day
are no less blasted in the tides of dust.
Why not take penmanship, ornithology?
Why not take you and me?

Can you give me of your
bare instincts enough? Save me
(though the cost may be beyond your ken)?
Do it then. For I know. But
I must know the full horoscope
of your desire. So give me
conjunctions of dust; make again
the knotted turning of the seasons start;
give me the whole fire of your heart.

Politics

1

They will win, I thought once,
because they have a myth.
The myth shapes their hunger.
And shapes also the faceless
beast made of many longings
who now coalesces in all of us
and surfaces crying 'Liberty!'

He is not good or evil. He is there, simply,
under the snow, under the white eye
of the dream continent
into which we sink further and further
an ancient pain grown ever more urgent
because we thought we left it behind
in Africa, Asia and Europe.

2

An almost monochrome snowscape
is the beginning of our myth.
Against it I have set
the brown and gold richness
of a room, a large room
with three large windows. Snow
flickers like cinema in all of them.

Hypnotic snow. Eradicating time
and banishing history from consciousness
you deceive us and begin us.
How shall we live with such blankness?
Shall we invoke the unjust past
or the equally false Utopian future?
Blood flows: a film on our eyes.

3

Riel, Mackenzie. My own ancestor,
Montgomery, declared to the judge

who sentenced him to hang: 'You think
you can send *me* to the gallows,
but *I* tell you that when
you're all frizzling with the devil,
I'll be keeping tavern on Yonge Street!'

He did too. First he was pardoned
and banished to British slave camps
in Van Diemen's Land. But he dug
himself out of Kingston's Fort Henry,
broke a leg, escaped to the States
half-starved, and was finally pardoned
to keep a mean tavern on Yonge Street.

4

That was the rough trade of our lives:
Riel hanged, Pierre Laporte strangled
in his own chain. History has many
unpleasant surprises for those
who placed her under a glass case labelled
conquest, cross, mosaic-piece, piece
of the peaceable future kingdom.

For now the dreamer wakes,
now the sleeper wakens into time,
and no mythology finally will matter
(theirs or ours) unless it is true
to a single room with its large windows
a single room made of many windows
opening and closing their eyes of cold snow.

JOHN NEWLOVE

b. 1938

I Talk to You

I talk to you (whispering and pointing
whatever it is I wish to know) and no-one
gives attention. Why should they?

The excessive sun has no intention.
It moves easily on, burning my skin.

To whom should I talk except
my exhaustive self? To whom indicate
the shape of the house I inhabit,
or the brain and the leg, the pressures
behind the bony skull, the leg's hairs,
the moulding of the front-door stairs.

To talk to myself expecting an answer,
expecting a credence, confessing
insaneness in this dialogue –

is this to be mad? To sound foolish,
to sound foolishness, to be mad to say,
to say the convulsive illegible world
is how? and demand a reply.

To be mad, to be mad, unangry, to sit
sour in the old wooden chair
and run across the unmoving world
without pity, with only the wild regret
at not to know? To be mad for an answer
knowing there is no answer, except
in peculiarities and particularities?

The chair: what sort of sunny wood
its back is made of; the leg's shape
and not the brain's. And whom to talk to:
and whether it is fit to whisper or to shout.

Good Company, Fine Houses

Good company, fine houses
and consequential people,
you will not turn me
into a tin factory.

I know where the lean and half
starved gods are hiding,
I have slept in their mountains.

I have slept among them,
in their mountains turning
nightmarishly between the rocks
and the reaching plants.

I have seen red eyes
on my throat from behind
every bush and waterfall,
greedy for blood.

Good company, fine people,
except for the shooting,
how much will your funerals cost

in your consequential houses?
I know where the god is
hiding, starved. I have slept
in the turning mountain.

White Lies

The winter shines, I think.
But it's summer now and I'm not home.
The sky is the colour of a pike's belly,
the air stinks. It is pretending
to be about to rain. The atmosphere
is heavy, is glue. Glum glue.

I seem to remember those winters.
The hard-surfaced snow

would have stretched tightly
over the low hills, vast pearls
glowing in the night of five o'clock,
white lies.

Bright cars cautious on the roads,
the grey skeleton trees, occasional greens,
rarely a rabbit's convulsive flash,
black birds sitting on telephone wires,
waiting, waiting.

I haven't been home for years.

The Double-Headed Snake

Not to lose the feel of the mountains
while still retaining the prairies
is a difficult thing. What's lovely
is whatever makes the adrenalin run;
therefore I count terror and fear among
the greatest beauty. The greatest
beauty is to be alive, forgetting nothing,
although remembrance hurts
like a foolish act, is a foolish act.

Beauty's whatever
makes the adrenalin run. Fear
in the mountains at night-time's
not tenuous, it is not the cold
that makes me shiver, civilized man,
white, I remember
the stories of the Indians,
Sis-i-utl, the double-headed snake.

Beauty's what makes
the adrenalin run. Fear at night
on the level plains, with no horizon
and the stars too bright, wind bitter
even in June, in winter
the snow harsh and blowing,

is what makes me
shiver, not the cold air alone.

And one beauty cancels another. The plains
seem secure and comfortable
at Crow's Nest Pass; in Saskatchewan
the mountains are comforting
to think of; among
the eastwardly diminishing hills
both the flatland and the ridge
seem easy to endure.

As one beauty
cancels another, remembrance
is a foolish act, a double-headed snake
striking in both directions, but I
remember plains and mountains, places
I come from, places I adhere and live in.

JOHN THOMPSON

1938–76

Coming Back

Night is day, winter a single
gust of wind which bangs
the moon;

the time it takes
to lift my hand to grasp
the smell of balsam

I break the buried rock
of an immense journey

and stand before the window
my eyes rimy
with frost, glittering
with owls' flights, my mouth
full of dead ferns;

around my wife's hand swirls
a mist of flour,
the hands of my daughter
gleam with paint,

and I come, simply, bringing
a few fir cones
which have lain for months
under the snow,

back to the quiet, knowing
those terrible iron tongues
no longer hammer
against the walls of my house.

Horse

Your great hooves sunk
    in red mud, massive,
        still, you stare out

over the edge of the world;
    small fires
        flare in your eyes;

the sun turns in hunger
    about your dark head,
        sniffing the earth in you,
tasting your smoke,

and waits for your thighs
    to shift, your hooves
        to strain from the ground,

for some speech from your black muscles:

so the earth would tilt
    under your weight,

hawks plummet upward, the dead
    float in the air like flies,

and we, thrown from our warm furrows,
    relearn our balance,
        reach out in the dark to test

our crooked new bones.

DAVID HELWIG

b.1938

The Jockeys

They live by their betrayed bodies,
they are boys with old faces, riding,
always riding the great muscled horses.
Day after day, bent like cripples,
they race the same long track.

They hold and rein in their horses
with small hands, or speed them on
with quick strokes of the thin crop.

Without them, the horses would not follow
the track, not race, but run only
to heat the air, galloping in arabesques,
wheeling and turning. Or would be still
as the wind shaped itself around their haunches.

The jockeys
ride the strong muscled horses
day after day
over the worn earth of the track.

Lot

should the pillar sing, should salt
talk aloud, it would be no wonder
in these days of miracles

in those cities
the frightened burghers gabbled
as the fire came down
to punish their inventive appetites

oh who would not look back
to the familiar cities

the giddy degenerate afternoons
the daily chatter

should the pillar speak, what wonder

and I return now to listen
here in the desert

remember the hot afternoons
when I licked the sweat from her skin

by the light of the falling fire I wait
and my tongue, remembering, reaches,
touches salt and is stung

The Death of Harlequin

I cannot say
why he should look
so like a broken bird
except that a pile of sticks
and a gaiety of rags
are his grave
and that his laughter
ran into the sky
and that his tears
flew upward
and that at his death
he dropped slowly
with a fine grace
in dying
and that his falling
brought distances into our eyes.

MARGARET ATWOOD

b. 1939

They are hostile nations

1

In view of the fading animals
the proliferation of sewers and fears
the sea clogging, the air
nearing extinction

we should be kind, we should
take warning, we should forgive each other

Instead we are opposite, we
touch as though attacking,

the gifts we bring
even in good faith maybe
warp in our hands to
implements, to manoeuvres

2

Put down the target of me
you guard inside your binoculars,
in turn I will surrender

this aerial photograph
(your vulnerable
sections marked in red)
I have found so useful

See, we are alone in
the dormant field, the snow
that cannot be eaten or captured

3

Here there are no armies
here there is no money

It is cold and getting colder

We need each others'
breathing, warmth, surviving
is the only war
we can afford, stay

walking with me, there is almost
time/if we can only
make it as far as

the (possibly) last summer

Notes from various pasts

Capsized somewhere and stranded
here, in a bluegrey rocking-chair
and having adjusted somewhat
to the differences in pressure

I sit, looking at
what has been caught in the net
this morning: messages
from a harsher level.

I rock on the bluegrey
day, while below me
the creatures of the most profound
ocean chasms are swimming
far under even the memory
of sun and tidal moon:

some of them fragile, some
vicious as needles; all
sheathed in an armoured skin
that is a language; camouflage
of cold lights, potent signals
that allure prey or flash
networks of warning
transmitted through the deep core
of the sea to each other only.

Have I gained eyes and lungs, freedom
to tell the morning from the night
to breathe
      Have I lost
an electric wisdom
in the thin marooning air?

The words lie washed ashore
on the margins, mangled
by the journey upwards to the bluegrey
surface, the transition:

these once-living
and phosphorescent meanings
fading in my hands

I try to but can't decipher

Variation on the Word Sleep

I would like to watch you sleeping,
which may not happen.
I would like to watch you,
sleeping. I would like to sleep
with you, to enter
your sleep as its smooth dark wave
slides over my head

and walk with you through that lucent
wavering forest of bluegreen leaves
with its watery sun & three moons
towards the cave where you must descend,
towards your worst fear

I would like to give you the silver
branch, the small white flower, the one
word that will protect you
from the grief at the center
of your dream, from the grief
at the center. I would like to follow

you up the long stairway
again & become
the boat that would row you back
carefully, a flame
in two cupped hands
to where your body lies
beside me, and you enter
it as easily as breathing in

I would like to be the air
that inhabits you for a moment
only. I would like to be that unnoticed
& that necessary.

GEORGE McWHIRTER

b. 1939

To Dona Isabel, Protectress of the Faith

Dona Isabel,
I must report
That on Sundays off San Felieu de Guixols,
Church bells clang
Like dead buckets in a well.

A shadow leaps from the upright stone
Of the cross,
And Peter laughs like a cockerel
While Christ spread-eagles,
Like a ruptured jaguar, on the sand.

Dona Isabel,
No hangknot jerks as Judas drops
To cool his bunions in the sea.

And Dona Isabel
What with their marrowless thoughts
And dried-up wits,
Old fogies diddle in their pews
And pray in urinals.
The young are stuffed with youngness.
Only doubt survives, dear Queen.

You remember doubt.
That parchment Columbus wrapped around his egg
And Galileo pinned to a black diamond
With a star.

Virgin

A slot parts level with her mouth. She
bites a wafer of light that glides through
the shutter, then another. She heaves the

cord which lies broad and flat against
her palm like the wick of a huge lamp.
The shutters rattle, each rib protesting
a resurrection.

He has risen.

Slowly, like oil, sweat dribbles into her armpit.

Reminder

A spider catches on the peak
of my cap while I paint. I let
it spin down to my chin and swivel up.

This year is crazed with insects:
– no snow to cut down their numbers in the killing
months.

Their instincts read it this way:
they have come into their own, inherited
cabin and garden; and this small brown

speckled weaver has deemed me obsolete.
It webs this image God made
in its gossamer. My eyes glint, sunken

with their staring, like lost water
in a well. Up and down; thither
and yon, the thin arcs and triangle sectored

into a multigram. I turn
my humour on the spider like a lamp, thank
it for midges and mosquitoes it will trap.

I compliment both workmanship and daring;
(yet have I ever thought I was not to be feared
by spiders – my finger
near them scuttled many. I tap
it on the rail as a reminder). Then,
slow

and persistent as the buzz around a bee
or, like the whistle
of our kettle when my wife is talking

and late with making tea, it pierces
my understanding.
I'm expecting it to stop.

Stop dead with these projections. Tip
some hypothetical cap. And
apologize.

When it refuses, I return to my very human
humour. I notice my wife by the azalea. I walk
out and stalk up behind ker. Knock

her on the shoulder. Seeing the fine
incarceration of my face, she screams.
I blow the web off with a kiss that clings.

PATRICK LANE

b. 1939

Wild Horses

Just to come once alone
to these wild horses
driving out of high Cascades,
raw legs heaving the hip-high snow.
Just once alone. Never to see
the men and their trucks.

Just once alone. Nothing moves
as the stallion with five free mares
rush into the guns. All dead.
Their eyes glaze with frost.
Ice bleeds in their nostrils
as the cable hauls them in.

Later, after the swearing
and the stamping of feet,
we ride down into Golden.

Quit bitchin.
It's a hard bloody life
and a long week
for three hundred bucks of meat.

That and the dull dead eyes
and the empty meadows.

Bunkhouse North

He played with his rifle
as if it was a woman;
shot the oiled bolt back and forth
with a neat

click/snap

and spent his sunday hours
aiming it at everything that moved
until the rest of us in the bunkhouse
twitched each time he softly murmured

pow

each of us remembering
deaths we had delivered:
the gutshot deer,
the stumbling bear
snapping at his leg to eat his pain,
the falling men pitching on the plain.

Each of us wishing he was blooded
or was wise in the loneliness
that comes across the eyes
in that cold quick moment
just after making love.

The Carpenter

The gentle fears he tells me of being
afraid to climb back down each day
from the top of the unfinished building.
He says: I'm getting old
and wish each morning when I arrive
I could beat into shape
a scaffold to take me higher
but the wood I'd need
is still growing on the hills
the nails raw red with rust
still changing shape in bluffs
somewhere north of my mind.

I've hung over this city like a bird
and seen it change from shacks to towers.
It's not that I'm afraid
but sometimes when I'm alone up here
and know I can't get higher
I think I'll just walk off the edge
and either fall or fly

and then he laughs
so that his plum-bob goes awry
and single strokes the spikes into the joists
pushing the floor another level higher
like a hawk who every year adds levels to his nest
until he's risen above the tree he builds on
and alone lifts off into the wind
beating his wings like nails into the sky.

DENNIS LEE

b. 1939

From *Civil Elegies*

2

Master and Lord, where
are you?
A man moves back and forth
between what must be done to save the world
and what will save his soul,
and neither is real. For many years
I could not speak your name, nor now but
even stilled at times by openings like
joy my whole life
aches, the streets I walk along to work declare
your absence, the headlines
declare it, the nation, and
over and over the harried lives I
watch and live with, holding my breath and
sometimes a thing rings true –
they all give way and declare your real absence.

Master and Lord,
let be. I can say
nothing about you that does not
vanish like tapwater.
I know
the world is not enough; a woman straightens
and turns from the sink and asks her life the
question, why should she
fake it? and after a moment she
shrugs, and returns to the sink. A man's
adrenalin takes hold, at a meeting he makes
his point, and pushes and sees that
things will happen now . . . and then in the pause he knows
there are endless things in the world and this is not for real.

Whatever is lovely, whatever deserves
contempt, whatever dies –
over and over, in every thing we meet
we meet that emptiness.

It is a homecoming, as men once knew
their lives took place in you.
And we cannot get on, no matter how we
rearrange our lives and we cannot let go for
then there is nothing at all.

Master and Lord, there was a
measure once.
There was a time when men could say
my life, my job, my home
and still feel clean.
The poets spoke of earth and heaven. There were no symbols.

6

I am one for whom the world is constantly proving too much –
not this nor that, but the continental drift to barbarian
normalcy frightens me, I am constantly
stiffening before my other foot touches the ground and numb in my
stance I hear the country pouring on past me gladly on all sides,
towed and protesting but pelting very fast downhill,
and though I do not decry technopolis I can see only the bread and
circuses to come,
and no man will use a mirror to shave, in case he
glimpse himself and abroad there will come obscenity, a senseless
procession of holy wars
and we will carry the napalm for our side, proud of our clean
hands.
I can't converse with friends without discussing Rome, this is
bad news and though the upshot is not that I am constantly
riddled with agonies my thing is often worse for I cannot get
purchase on life.

You Can Climb Down Now

Forgive me that I
ask too much of your
body,
boosting sweet day-to-day flesh into
Endless Redemption by Passion.
Must be a
drag up there, and you can
climb down now.

If only something could
centre us.
One
whiff of carnal joy and a man will come unhinged,
or try to cram the body of his longing
thru somebody's flesh into
heaven,
to never be lonesome again.

Aw, you must get
tired up there, those crummy wings & you
don't look good in marble.
You can climb
down now, girl, I
like you more in person – though I
willed you there. I
nailed you there.
Forgive me.

bill bissett

b. 1939

wer they angels i didint know

sum uv them had wings but
not all uv them nd sum had long
hair nd sum had shortr hair
nd most uv them wer wearing robes

i was staring at th sky from th mouth
uv th cave sumtimes i still heer
them espeshully in th morning whn i
first get up ther voices practising crescendo
chorus or humming with baritone up nd
down riffs   ther wer ribbons from
them streeming nd attachd to
thos uv all colors wer horses
running a chariot with guys
riding th reins uv th steeds
nd from bhind th chariot mor
ribbons agen uv all colors

lifting th sun up ovr th horizon

trumpets whirling wind th sky
was filld with sound   how dew

yu think th sun cums up

what wud yu say to ths dreem

duz it hold yu or bettr let yu

its pollushun alert in seattul today

heer yu cant see very far at nite
duz it mattr tho if yu find love
duz our inabilitee to dew sumthing abt
th pollushun or any othr commershul for

serious politikul problems make it easy
to leev what love we find

if yu dew it in a pome is that doing it

as well as not telling peopul thers evn an alert
in vankouver theyve decidid not to advise
heart nd lung patients to stay indoors
during ths time evn tho th scale is 11
points above dangrous bcoz th worry mite
make them wors   bettr they shud brave
th smog nd if they die in it at leest they
wont know why   isint that rite   th news
abt th pollushun didint evn leek out til almost
a week aftr it reechd th 11 points above
dangrous   how many points above we
ar all ded is it now

i can only record what i know

wo

get it togethr in time for what
is cumming yu ar not th centr
uv th world each time yu bow yr
spirit to th wind yu acknowledg
that tho yu fill th holy void
with yr words nd wishes what
fills yu is anothr prson in
spirit or in prson th warmth
nd flesh nd company inside th
music we make nd share togethr
within a fast nd fleeting dawn

bill bissett

th guy drivin round in

th vankouvr city pound
truck is giving me
sum strange
looks
so i
barkd at
him

DAVID SOLWAY

b. 1941

The Lame Diver

The currents buoy him up, the soft pressures
turn his twisted bones to iron. He knows
miracles are transient, and secures
the black discrepancy of the airhose.

The sea is a shoulder he can lean on,
a faith, greave or leg-brace, propping up knees.
The seaweed sways like a church of women
at their prayers calling down epiphanies.

And ropes of light reeve through coral and sponge,
plunge from the blue hull of heaven that floats
above him. Cities appear. Mermaids lunge.
Seahorses curtsey in bright redingotes.

Now that gravity's unshackled his feet
the diver moves across the deep earth's fault;
outstripping his body like an athlete
he casts his crutch over his back like salt.

The Cable

Come to cove, they let the anchor fall,
and to the winch's reassuring sound
the gulls reply in their colloquial.
The sea is calm for all the miles around –

cameo or snapshot, if not for wind
that shoves and muscles in its parable.
The anchor holds the seabed as designed.
Faithfully, the yacht swings round its cable.

The Last Supper

What did they talk about
around that wrecked, angular table?
How did they manage a conversation
that had been going on for years
in a vernacular of miracles,
seemingly undistracted by that gaudy halo
(or had they grown accustomed to it
   as a loose-fitting wig
   worn to subvert the dust,
   or just another kind of stetson)?

The problem surely must have been
how to sustain a dialogue
of epigram & parable,
prophecy & confession,
meal after meal year after year
with never a dirty joke, a vulgar reference,
or the salt & leaven of blasphemy
to lighten that attention.

O all those pale blond apostles
but mainly
sneaking Judas in the corner
hungry for the human touch . . .

GWENDOLYN MACEWEN

b. 1941

The Thing Is Violent

Self, I want you now to be
violent and without history,
for we've rehearsed too long our ceremonial ballet
and I fear my calm against your exquisite rage.

I do not fear that I will go mad
but that I may not, and the shadows of my sanity
blacken out your burning; act once
and you need not act again –
give me no ceremony, scars are not pain.

The thing is violent, nothing precedes it,
it has no meaning before or after –
sweet wounds which burn like stars,
stigmata of the self's own holiness,
appear and plot new zodiacs upon the flesh.

The Child Dancing

there's no way I'm going to write about
the child dancing in the Warsaw ghetto
in his body of rags

there were only two corpses
on the pavement that day
and the child I will not write about
had a face as pale and trusting
as the moon

(so did
the boy with a green belly full of dirt
lying by the roadside
in a novel of Kazantzakis

and the small girl T. E. Lawrence wrote about
whom they found after the Turkish massacre
with one shoulder chopped off, crying:
'don't *hurt* me, Baba!')

I don't feel like slandering them with poetry.

the child who danced
in the Warsaw ghetto
to some music no one else could hear
had moon-eyes, no
green horror and no fear
but something worse

a simple desire to please
the people who stayed
to watch him shuffle back and forth,
his feet wrapped in the newspapers
of another ordinary day

Inside the Great Pyramid

all day the narrow shaft
received us; everyone
came out sweating and
gasping for air, and one
old man collapsed
upon a stair;
                    I thought:
the fact that it has stood
so long
is no guarantee
it will stand today,
but went in anyway
and heard when I was
halfway up a long
low rumbling like
the echo of ancient stones

first straining to their place;
                    I thought:
we have made this, we
have made *this*.
I scrambled out into
the scandalous sun and saw
the desert was an hourglass
we had forgotten to invert,
a tasselled camel falling
to his knees, the River
filling the great waterclock
of earth.

Cairo, 1966

Tall Tales

From *the T. E. Lawrence Poems*

It has been said that I sometimes lie, or bend the truth
    to suit me. Did I make that four hundred mile
    trip alone in Turkish territory or not?
    I wonder if it is anybody's business
    to know. Syria is still there,
    and the long lie that the war was.

Was there a poster of me offering money for my capture
    and did I stand there staring at myself,
    daring anyone to know me? Consider
    truth and untruth, consider why they call them
    the *theatres* of war. All of us
    played our roles to the hilt.

Poets only play with words, you know; they too
    are masters of the Lie, the Grand Fiction.
    Poets and men like me who fight for something
    contained in words, but not words.

What if the whole show was a lie, and it bloody well was –
    would I still lie to you? Of course I would.

DOUG BEARDSLEY

b. 1941

Inside Passage

Good morning.

The lead dawn dayless drizzle
comes on us like Drake, sailing from Mexico,
he never reached as far as
New Albion, safe for the Salish, Kwakiutl & the candle-fish.

Tragedy belongs by right to such a place,
rivers the mist, slips like a hand
over the green headland, a few decrepit cabins,
clumps of fir, hemlocked pattern
of blue seas & peaks 6000 feet and climbing.

Sheer rock walls bluff the river,
cubical blocks stand up in midstream,
and the waters below in the channel so
constricted, even the gulls give up on us.

We turn in, trying to find the passage through.

Natural Selection

For nine weeks now I've watched them
Grow to perfection in the sun.
I've seen sights too incredible to tell,
I've been through the whole harrowing thing,
From bud to blossom, through flower,
To green pellet no bigger than your thumb.

It's an astounding process, but now and then
A wind comes up out of nowhere
And sends shivers through the leaves.
The great mellow growths make a cracking noise

That scares the hell out of me
The way they fall, like a ledge giving in.

I rush to save them, but it's not much use.
They blow away like baseballs, like some high fly
Drifting from an anxious fielder, but I'm not upset.
Cradling the bruised-brown things
I can see where the worm's made them weak,
Drilled them sure as death, straight through.

Unlike the worm, I select the ripest ones.
The first bite's the best.
You don't know what you're missing.

Birdbath

Each morning I fill the bath with fresh water

The bloody birds come and collect on the edge
The first one in splashes about
He leaves his turd and feathers behind

The others dont mind
Two hide in the bush hoping to sneak out
The smaller ones wait their turn on the wall

Sometimes you cant see the trees for birds
When they get on my nerves I step on a worm
This sort of thing goes on all day

We fly south in September

DON McKAY

b. 1942

March Snow

The snow is sick. The pure
page breaks and greys and
drools around the edges, sucks
at my snowshoe every heavy step saying
fuck it, just
fuck it, softly to itself.

It fails the toothpaste test.
In fact, it makes me think of dentists
frowning, the sag along the jawline as he
hmm as he
mutters something to his nurse
whose complexion's turned to cottage cheese
from too much Harlequin Romance.

So is it possible to
fix a person to her place, to pin her
like a name tag to her
self.
I missed
the atomic fission of her yearning till I looked back

bang into a fiery lake: the snow
suicidal with desire, wearing
his image like a poster of the movie star
she dies to be   the sun
simmering in her flesh her
nerves her burning
bedroom eyes

too bright for mine.
Beside the house scared earth emerges
frawny with sleep, imagines
the atrocity of tulips thrusting up
dog-penis red and raw.

Alias Rock Dove, Alias Holy Ghost

How come you don't see more dead pigeons?
Because when they die their bodies turn to lost gloves
and get swept up by the city sweepers. Even so
their soft inconsequence can sabotage a jumbo jet
the way a flock of empty details
devastates a marriage.

Someone down the hall is working on an epic cough.
Another makes it to the bathroom
yet again, groping past my door. All night
the senile plumbing interviews itself: some war or other.
The faint sweet smell of must.

Along the ledges of the parking garage they flutter
wanly as the grey blue residue of nightmares.
Softness of bruises, of sponges
sopping up exhaust.

City poets try to read their tracks along the windowsill for some
announcement. Such as our concrete palaces
have the consistency of cake. Such as
Metropolis of Crumbs. Such as
Save us, Christ, the poor sons of bitches.

Pool

Early deepshadowed pool we come
on tip-toe to your whispers of fish, to flick
these flies, sol-fa,
                    touching
exactly on your surface.

The real flies hang
ardent in air
full of their own small destinies
vivid with undelivered news –

but wait:
let us enter with ritual
flexings of elbow and shoulder, let us know your
delicate contingency as virgins vaguely
deeply stirred would know

that somewhere in their sleep
the sleek trout lurk.

MICHAEL ONDAATJE

b. 1943

White Dwarfs

This is for people who disappear
for those who descend into the code
and make their room a fridge for Superman
– who exhaust costume and bones that could perform flight,
who shave their moral so raw
they can tear themselves through the eye of a needle
this is for those people
that hover and hover
and die in the ether peripheries

There is my fear
of no words   of
falling without words
over and over   of
mouthing the silence
Why do I love most
among my heroes those
who sail to that perfect edge
where there is no social fuel
Release of sandbags
to understand their altitude –

that silence of the third cross
3rd man hung so high and lonely
we dont hear him say
say his pain, say his unbrotherhood
What has he to do with the smell of ladies
can they eat off his skeleton of pain?

The Gurkhas in Malaya
cut the tongues of mules
so they were silent beasts of burden
in enemy territories
after such cruelty what could they speak of anyway
And Dashiell Hammett in success

suffered conversation and moved
to the perfect white between the words

This white that can grow
is fridge, bed,
is an egg – most beautiful
when unbroken, where
what we cannot see is growing
in all the colours we cannot see

there are those burned out stars
who implode into silence
after parading in the sky
after such choreography what would they wish to speak of anyway

We're at the graveyard

Stuart Sally Kim and I
watching still stars
or now and then sliding stars
like hawk spit to the trees.
Up there the clear charts,
the systems' intricate branches
which change with hours and solstices,
the bone geometry of moving from there, to there.
And down here – friends
whose minds and bodies
shift like acrobats to each other.
When we leave, they move
to an altitude of silence.

So our minds shape
and lock the transient,
parallel these bats
who organize the air
with thick blinks of travel.
Sally is like grey snow in the grass.
Sally of the beautiful bones
pregnant below stars.

Song to Alfred Hitchcock and Wilkinson

Flif flif flif flif very fast
is the noise the birds make
running over us.
A poet would say 'fluttering',
or
'see-sawing with sun on their wings'.
But all it is
is flif flif flif flif very fast.

Country Night

The bathroom light burns over the mirror

In the blackness of the house
beds groan from the day's exhaustion
hold the tired shoulders bruised
and cut legs the unexpected
3 a.m. erections. Someone's dream
involves a saw someone's
dream involves a woman.
We have all dreamed of finding the lost dog.

The last light on upstairs
throws a circular pattern
through the decorated iron vent
to become a living room's moon.

The sofa calls the dog, the cat
in perfect blackness walks over the stove.
In the room of permanent light
cockroaches march on enamel.
The spider with jewel coloured thighs the brown moth
with corporal stripes
                                        ascend pipes
and look into mirrors.

All night the truth happens.

SEYMOUR MAYNE

b. 1944

Before Passover

Before Passover there in the old flat
who searched at the underside of curtains,
spiders' dust, for the crumbs of final dinners?

Rummaging for bread in 1919
grandmother gave up on fresh compost heaps,
found instead sweetgrass
roots to feed her brood.

Later in the bustling capital the refugees
found others even trying
to cheat them of the price of passage.

'In Canada bread grows on trees –'
the children fed their big eyes and ears –
'In Canada one merely picks them for the eating!'

Early winter nights later in Montreal
they returned from work and underpay,
their snowy three-sided shadows
marching them into silence.

From afar now hear
the voices of aging women,
smell the shawl hugging
the wizened *bobeh*
who never begged but lived
for the conceptions of the ordinary,
bartering in the bazaars of genes and death.

Birthday

for Shulamit Nardi

Fallen in the Jewish Wars
a young man who will never age
shares the same prayerful eyes
of ancestors and our common birth
this day of May
– spring's point of no return
Son and brother still he lies
beneath shrubs and lettered stone
Though unknown to me his name
is on his father's lips,
his face before his mother
Today, our day, celebrating
my right hand has not forgotten
the cunning promise of script

CHARLES LILLARD

b. 1944

One View from the Kynoch

There were three eagles off the Kynoch's stone face.

We were drilling at the forty foot level;
we were drilling conglomerate;
our benchers rocked on their studs in the sluffing stone,
the bits screamed against the living rock,
and we sagged deeper into our boots praying for dusk.

All day those eagles hung off the palisades,
like gliders or islands in a stream;
all day
they swung through the fine air, swaying.

We swore we were cutting the rock of ages,
we swore and that only made it worse;
the day was in no hurry to go anywhere,
the mosquitoes hunted like hungry hawks.
In the cold stream we wrung the pain from our wrists,
felt the silence once again,
it was nightfall, the diesels were dead.
Once again we knew
    how far we were from our own voices.

And the eagles were still there –
three shadows streaking the palisades.
They will be here forever
    while men like ourselves
come and go, and all our mauling
will leave no more trace than a spray of sunbeams.
This is a pain which cannot be wrung out in a freshet.
This is bedrock;
    eagles will dance forever in the unwinding wind.

A Small Death in the Afternoon

I

We found this one
slim scribbler, there
should've been more;
a waterfall – fast water,
a deep pool for our fly
to wasp over . . . well
this will teach us
to reread certain creeks.

II

All day the day turned
against us
clumping upstream fighting
a current of devil's club,
willow tangles and vine maple;
we were trying to read
the stream,
those words fish leave
on the surface of soft water.

III

Such a small death,
just as it had been a
small life;
not one, certainly not one,
you could warm your hands over,
and it lay there beating by itself
among the grey pebbles.

Lakend/Cragg

It was on the southern drainage.
It was in the middle of July.
        At noon we broke through
the raspberry and foxglove,
        the potholes were where we'd left them,
                their vacant eyes a staring blue;
        the sun on our shoulders
                hotter than the hubs of hell.

Remember the devil's club – how we stood
on the rocks
picking the spines from my arm,
the dogs foraging in the seepage,
how, laughing,
we shed our clothes
and fell,
        into that bluest of skies?

PETER VAN TOORN

b. 1944

Ode

My snoweyed country
jabbed
with plenty
pine, maple, oak, ash, apple, fir, cedar, tamarack
stuffing a poet's belly, stuffing
the poet in any man
his belly for weather, mountains, water
friction in colours.
Take the dapper little towns
that stud the countryside by the railway lines
where grasses sting the sun
in thick fast greens
where you can see a pony, beech-coloured
grunching on alfalfa
with grass enough for years to come.
Where fields
are divided and undivided by rockpiles
neatly or grossly
as nature and community vary. Then that
dip in the bluff
that hundred foot gouge
in the trackside's dinosaur shoulders.
Or the stray lone houses
the blue lapstrake one on the burned down hill
surrounded by dandelions
and ducks
the typical letterlonely house
with its graveyard of cars
two generations back.
Snoweyed country
surly over flag debates, fishing rights
lost bomber contracts
loved
like a foal with its nose in the grass.

TOM WAYMAN

b. 1945

Picketing Supermarkets

Because all this food is grown in the store
do not take the leaflet.
Cabbages, broccoli and tomatoes
are raised at night in the aisles.
Milk is brewed in the rear storage areas.
Beef produced in vats in the basement.
Do not take the leaflet.
Peanut butter and soft drinks
are made fresh each morning by store employees.
Our oranges and grapes
are so fine and round
that when held up to the lights they cast no shadow.
Do not take the leaflet.

And should you take one
do not believe it.
This chain of stores has no connection
with anyone growing food someplace else.
How could we have an effect on local farmers?
Do not believe it.

The sound here is Muzak, for your enjoyment.
It is not the sound of children crying.
There *is* a lady offering samples
to mark Canada Cheese Month.
There is no dark-skinned man with black hair beside her
wanting to show you the inside of a coffin.
You would not have to look if there was.
And there are no Nicaraguan heroes
in any way connected with the bananas.

Pay no attention to these people.
The manager is a citizen.
All this food is grown in the store.

Unemployment

The chrome lid of the coffee pot
twists off, and the glass knob rinsed.
Lift out the assembly, dump
the grounds out. Wash the pot and
fill with water, put everything back with
fresh grounds and snap the top down.
Plug in again and wait.

Unemployment is also
a great snow deep around the house
choking the street, and the City.
Nothing moves. Newspaper photographs
show the traffic backed up for miles.
Going out to shovel the walk
I think how in a few days the sun will clear this.
No one will know I worked here.

This is like whatever I do.
How strange that so magnificent a thing as a body
with its twinges, its aches
should have all that chemistry, that bulk
the intricate electrical brain
subjected to something as tiny
as buying a postage stamp.
Or selling it.

Or waiting.

Wayman in Love

At last Wayman gets the girl into bed.
He is locked in one of those embraces
so passionate his left arm is asleep
when suddenly he is bumped in the back.
'Excuse me,' a voice mutters, thick with German.
Wayman and the girl sit up astounded
as a furry gentleman in boots and a frock coat
climbs in under the covers.

'My name is Doktor Marx,' the intruder announces
settling his neck comfortably on the pillow.
'I'm here to consider for you the cost of a kiss.'
He pulls out a notepad. 'Let's see now,
we have the price of the mattress, this room must be rented,
your time off work, groceries for two,
medical fees in case of accidents . . .'

'Look,' Wayman says,
'couldn't we do this later?'
The philosopher sighs, and continues: 'You are affected too, Miss.
If you are not working, you are going to resent
your dependent position. This will influence
I assure you, your most intimate moments . . .'

'Doctor, please,' Wayman says. 'All we want
is to be left alone.'
But another beard, more nattily dressed,
is also getting into the bed.
There is a shifting and heaving of bodies
as everyone wriggles out room for themselves.
'I want you to meet a friend from Vienna,'
Marx says. 'This is Doktor Freud.'

The newcomer straightens his glasses,
peers at Wayman and the girl.
'I can see,' he begins,
'that you two have problems . . .'

ROBERT BRINGHURST

b. 1946

Xenophanes

Earth is the ultimate substance.
What is, is made out of earth. We
who climb free of it,
milkthistles, mallards and men,
are made out of earth which is driven by water.

I have found chiton shells high
in the mountains, the finprints of fish
in the stonecutter's stone, and seen
boulders and trees dragged to sea
by the river. Water and earth
lurch, wrestle and twist in their purposeless
war, of which we
are a consequence, not an answer.

⋆

The earth gives birth to the sun
each morning, and washes herself in the water,
and slits the sun's throat every night
with a splintered stone, and washes
herself once again in the water.

Some days the sun, like a fattening
goose, crosses over in ignorant stupor.
Other days, watch: you will see him
shudder and twitch, like a rabbit
caught in the snare – but what
does it matter? One way
or the other, his death is the same.

We must learn to be thought
by the gods, not to think them.
Not to think gods have two eyes and ten fingers,
thirty-two teeth and two
asymmetrical footprints. Not to think
here in the unstoppered bowls

of our skulls we hold luminous
godbreath. The mush in our skulls
is compiled, like our toenails,
of rocksalt and silt, which is matted
like felt in the one case, and swollen
like hope in the other:

What is, is earth. What dies
is earth driven by water.

★

The earth has one end. It is under
our feet. You may think
differently; I am convinced
there is no other.

Essay on Adam

There are five possibilities. One: Adam fell.
Two: he was pushed. Three: he jumped. Four:
he only looked over the edge, and one look silenced him.
Five: nothing worth mentioning happened to Adam.

The first, that he fell, is too simple. The fourth,
fear, we have tried and found useless. The fifth,
nothing happened, is dull. The choice is between:
he jumped or was pushed. And the difference between these

is only an issue of whether the demons
work from the inside out or from the outside
in: the one
theological question.

Poem about Crystal

Look at it, stare
into the crystal because
it will tell you, not
the future, no, but
the quality of crystal,
clarity's nature,
teach you the stricture
of uncut, utterly
uncluttered light.

Biographical Notes

ACORN, MILTON: b. 1923 at Charlottetown, Prince Edward Island; served during World War II then worked as a carpenter; sold his tools to become a full-time poet; received the Governor General's Award for poetry in 1975. His selected poems, *Dig Up My Heart*, were published in 1983.

AMABILE, GEORGE: b. 1936 in New Jersey; educated at Universities of Minnesota and Connecticut; a founding editor of *The Far Point* and *Northern Light*. Has written several volumes of poetry, the latest being *The Presence of Fire*, 1982.

ANDERSON, PATRICK (1915–79): b. in England; educated at Oxford and Columbia. Came to Montreal in 1940 where he taught and was active in the 'Preview' group of writers. His selected poems, *Return to Canada*, appeared in 1977.

ATWOOD, MARGARET: b. 1939 in Ottawa; educated at University of Toronto and Radcliffe College; is published internationally, both as a novelist and as a poet. Her first full-length book of poems, *The Circle Game*, 1966, won the Governor General's Award. *Selected Poems* appeared in 1976 and *True Stories* in 1981.

AVISON, MARGARET: b. 1918 at Galt, Ontario; educated at the University of Toronto. Has worked at various times as secretary and librarian. *Sunblue* appeared in 1978 and her *Winter Sun* and *The Dumb founding* are published together in The Modern Canadian Poets series.

BAILEY, ALFRED G.: b. 1905 in Quebec City, educated in Fredericton, Toronto and London, England. Professor Emeritus of History at the University of New Brunswick. Has published several books of poetry, *Thanks for a Drowned Island* in 1973.

BEARDSLEY, DOUG: b. 1941 in Montreal, educated at the University of Victoria and York University, Toronto; is now a design and editing service partner in Victoria, B.C. Has written several volumes of poetry, the latest being *Kissing the Body of My Lord*, 1982.

BIRNEY, EARLE: b. 1904 in Calgary, Alberta; educated at the Universities of British Columbia, Toronto, California and London. Recipient of many honours; a continuing creative force as lecturer, essayist and reader. His first collection of poems was *David and Other Poems* (1942), his *Collected Poems* appeared in 1975 and there have been several selected appearances.

bissett, bill: b. 1939 in Halifax, moved to Vancouver and is associated with the blewointment press. Painter and concrete and sound poet; author of many works. His selected poems, *Beyond Even Faithful Legends*, appeared in 1980; his latest volume, *seagull on yonge street*, 1983.

BOWERING, GEORGE: b. 1935, Penticton, B.C.; educated at University of British Columbia; now professor at Simon Fraser University. A founding editor of *Tish* and author of books of criticism, novels and poetry, his selected poetry appearing in *West Window* in 1982.

BREWSTER, ELIZABETH: b. 1922, Chipman, N. B. Educated at University of New Brunswick and University of London. Professor at the University of Saskatchewan. She is a writer of fiction; *Sometimes I Think of Moving*, a book of poems, appeared in 1977.

BRINGHURST, ROBERT: b. 1946 in Los Angeles, raised in the Canadian Rockies; has travelled widely and written a number of books of poetry; his selected poems, *The Beauty of the Weapons*, was published in 1982. He lives in Vancouver.

CAMERON, GEORGE FREDERICK (1854–85): b. at New Glasgow, Nova Scotia; educated at Boston University and Queen's University. For the last three years of his life he was editor of the Kingston *News*. His selected poems, *Lyrics on Freedom, Love and Death*, appeared posthumously in 1887.

CAMPBELL, WILFRED (1858–1918): b. at Kitchener, Ontario; educated at Toronto and Cambridge, Massachusetts. Ran a literary column, *At the Mermaid Tavern*, in the Toronto *Globe* with Lampman and Duncan Campbell Scott. Worked in the Civil Service, Ottawa. *The Poetical Works of Wilfred Campbell* appeared in 1922.

CARMAN, BLISS (1861–1929): b. Fredericton, N.B.; educated there, and after post-graduate work at Edinburgh and Harvard, entered journalism in New York City. Lived for many years in New Canaan, Connecticut. Published many volumes of verse, the first, *Low Tide on Grand Pré*, appearing in 1893. He was related to Emerson, and was a cousin of Charles G. D. Roberts. *The Selected Poems of Bliss Carman*, edited by Lorne Pierce, was published in 1954.

COHEN, LEONARD: b. 1934 in Montreal; educated at McGill University; post-graduate work at Columbia. Internationally known as a composer-singer. *Selected Poems* appeared in a recent edition in The Modern Canadian Poets series. Author of two novels: *The Favourite Game*, 1963, and *Beautiful Losers*, 1966.

COLES, DON: b. 1928 in Woodstock, Ontario. He has lived and studied in Cambridge, Florence, Scandinavia and Central Europe. He is now in Humanities Division at York University, Toronto. He has written three volumes of poetry, the latest, *The Prinzhorn Collection*, 1982.

CRAWFORD, ISABELLA VALANCY (1850–87): b. in Dublin; the family migrated to Ontario when the poet was eight. Lived with her mother in Toronto in humble circumstances, writing indefatigably until her death at the age of thirty-six. The *Collected Poems* appeared in 1905.

DRUMMOND, WILLIAM HENRY (1854–1907): 'The Poet of the Habitant' was born near Mohill, Ireland. Attended McGill and Bishop's University; established a physician's practice at Stornoway, later in Knowlton and Montreal. His *Complete Poems* was published in 1926.

DUDEK, LOUIS: b. 1918 in Montreal; educated at McGill and Columbia; is on the Faculty of English at McGill University. Was a partner in Contact Press, Toronto, editor of *Delta* magazine and Delta Press and the McGill Poetry series. His *Collected Poetry* appeared in 1971; is engaged in an experimental poem without prescribed conclusion, the first part *Continuation I* being published in 1981.

EVERSON, R. G.: b. 1903 in Oshawa, Ontario. Has been writing poetry since 1920, his first book, *Three Dozen Poems*, appearing in 1957, his *Selected Poems* in 1970 and a further volume, *Herd of Stars*, in 1983

FIAMENGO, MARYA: b. 1926 in Vancouver of Serbo-Croatian heritage. Educated at the University of British Columbia where she now teaches. Her latest volume of poetry, new and selected, *North of the Cold Star*, appeared in 1978.

FINCH, ROBERT: b. 1900 at Freeport, Long Island; educated at the University of Toronto and the Sorbonne. For many years professor of French at the University of Toronto. He has won the Governor General's Award for poetry twice. His latest volume, *Has and Is*, appeared in 1981.

FORD, R. A. D.: b. 1915 in Ottawa; educated at the University of Western Ontario and Cornell. For many years Canadian Ambassador to the Soviet Union; now retired and living in France. Has made distinguished translations from Spanish and Russian poets, and has published several volumes of verse; a *Selected* collection appeared in 1983.

GLASSCO, JOHN (1909–81): b. in Montreal and educated at McGill University. Translated *The Journal of Saint-Denys-Garneau*, 1962, and edited *The Poetry of French Canada in Translation*, 1970. His prose includes *Memoirs of Montparnasse*, 1970, and *The Fatal Woman*, 1974. His *Selected Poems* appeared in 1971.

GOLDSMITH, OLIVER (1794–1861): b. at St Andrew's, New Brunswick. Entered government service and became Deputy Commissary General, serving in Canada and abroad. He was a grandnephew of the author of *The Deserted Village*, the prototype for his own *The Rising Village* published in England 1825 and in a revised Canadian text, 1834.

GRIER, ELDON: b. 1917 in London, England; educated in Montreal. Well-known artist now resident on the west coast. His *Selected Poems* appeared in 1971 and a further collection, *Assassination of Colour*, in 1978.

GUSTAFSON, RALPH: b. 1909 in the Eastern Townships of Quebec; educated at Bishop's University and at Oxford; retired from Bishop's as professor and Poet in Residence in 1979. Since 1942 has edited revisions of this book; music critic. His *Fire on Stone* (1974) won the Governor General's Award and his selected poems 1944–83 were published under the title *The Moment Is All*.

HEAVYSEGE, CHARLES (1816–76): b. in Huddersfield, England, came to Montreal in 1853 where he worked as a cabinet-maker and journalist. A poetic drama, *Saul* (1857, revised 1869) won international attention; this was followed by *Count Filippo; or, The Unequal Marriage* in 1860 and by several books of poetry. (The sections from *Saul* here given are to be found as follows: Malzah's soliloquy in the grounds of Saul's palace, Third Part, Act I, sc. V. Saul's soliloquies at Endor and the Hebrew Camps, Third Part, Act VI, sc. VII. The selection from *Count Filippo* is from Act IV, sc. VII. The song occurs in Act II, sc. V.)

HELWIG, DAVID: b. 1938 in Toronto, educated at the Universities of Toronto and Liverpool; author of novels, a collection of short stories and several volumes of poetry gathered in *The Sign of the Gunman*, 1968, with a later book of *Atlantic Crossings*, 1977. He is a member of the English Department at Queen's University, Kingston, Ontario.

HERBIN, JOHN FREDERIC (1860–1923): b. Windsor, Nova Scotia; educated at Acadia University. Lived as a jeweller in Wolfville, N.S. His books of poems are *Canada and Other Poems*, 1891, and *The Marshlands*, 1899.

JOHNSON, PAULINE (1861–1913): b. at Stratford, Ontario, daughter of an Englishwoman and a Mohawk chief. She adopted the Mohawk name Tekahionwake and gave concert readings in Canada, the United States and England. *Flint and Feather*, her collected poems, appeared in 1912.

JOHNSTON, GEORGE: b. 1913, Hamilton, Ontario; educated at University of Toronto, now retired as professor at Carleton University in Ottawa. *Happy Enough*, 1972, collected previous books together with new poems and a further selection, *Auk Redivivus*, came out in 1981.

JONAS, GEORGE: b. 1935 in Budapest, Hungary. Since 1957 has lived in Toronto, working for the Canadian Broadcasting Corporation and freelancing. Has published three books of poetry, the latest, *Cities*, 1973.

JONES, D. G.: b. 1929 at Bancroft, Ontario; educated at McGill and Queen's Universities. Professor at l'Université de Sherbrooke. Has published a study of themes and images in Canadian literature, *Butterfly on Rock*, 1970, and several books of poems, the latest being *A Throw of Particles*, 1983, new and selected poems.

KEARNS, LIONEL: b. 1937 in Nelson, B.C., and educated at the University of British Columbia; presently in the department of English at Simon Fraser University. His new and selected poems, *Ignoring the Bomb*, came out in 1982.

KENNEDY, LEO: b. 1907 in Liverpool, England; educated in Montreal and lived in the United States as an advertising writer. His first book, *The Shrouding* (1933) was re-issued in 1975.

KLEIN, A. M. (1909–72): b. in Montreal and educated there; practised law until his retirement in 1954. *The Collected Poems* appeared in 1974. He is also the author of a novel, *The Second Scroll*, 1951.

KNISTER, RAYMOND (1899–1932): b. near Comber, Ontario, and educated at Trinity College, Toronto. Was on the staff of *The Midland* in the United States, then returned to Toronto, freelance writing. His premature death was by drowning. His *Collected Poems* was published in 1949 and the *Selected Stories* in 1974.

KROETSCH, ROBERT: b. 1927 in Heisler, Alberta, educated at the Universities of Alberta, McGill and Iowa; a writer in residence at Canadian universities, author of several novels, winning the Governor General's Award for *The Studhorse Man* (1969); and several collections of poems.

LAMPMAN, ARCHIBALD (1861–99): b. at Morpeth, Ontario, and educated at Trinity College, Toronto. From 1883 on he was in the Post Office Department of the Civil Service, Ottawa. In 1974 appeared

The Poems of Archibald Lampman, including the Memoir by his friend, Duncan Campbell Scott, and poems from unpublished manuscripts, *At the Long Sault*, originally published in 1943.

LANE, PATRICK: b. 1939 in Nelson, B.C.; worked at a variety of jobs in construction, logging; moved to Vancouver, became involved in the founding of Very Stone House Press; writer in residence at various Canadian universities. *Poems New & Selected* appeared in 1978.

LANIGAN, GEORGE T. (1846–86): b. Three Rivers, Quebec. Founded the *Montreal Star* newspaper. His *Fables Out of the World* appeared in 1887.

LAYTON, IRVING: b. 1912 in Rumania; educated at McGill University; associated with Dudek and Souster in founding Contact Press. Has published numerous volumes of poetry, winning the Governor General's Award and representing Canada at poetry festivals in many countries; has taught at several Canadian universities. The collected poems, *A Wild Peculiar Joy*, appeared in 1982.

LEE, DENNIS: b. 1939 in Toronto, studied at the University of Toronto and has taught there and at York University; co-founder of the House of Anansi Press. A publisher's consultant and full-time poet and critic; his collections of poems for children are famous; the latest collection of adult poetry is *The Gods* (1979).

LE PAN, DOUGLAS: b. 1914 at Toronto; educated at Toronto and Oxford; has held many diplomatic and university positions. His novel, *The Deserter*, appeared in 1964, and his two collections of poetry, *The Wounded Prince*, in 1948, and *The Net and the Sword* which won the Governor General's Award, in 1953.

LESLIE, KENNETH (1892–1974): b. at Pictou, Nova Scotia; educated at Dalhousie, Nebraska and Harvard universities. *The Poems of Kenneth Leslie* was published in 1971.

LILLARD, CHARLES: b. 1944 in California, grew up in Alaska, worked in the bush there and in British Columbia. He has taught at the University of Victoria and is now freelancing. His fifth book of poetry is *A Coastal Range*, 1983.

LIVESAY, DOROTHY: b. 1909 in Winnipeg; educated at the University of Toronto and the Sorbonne. Active in many literary movements as an editor and writer in residence at Canadian universities. She has written memoirs and her *Collected Poems: The Two Seasons* was published in 1972.

LOWRY, MALCOLM (1909–57): b. Merseyside, England; educated at Cambridge. Lived from 1939 until 1954 mainly in a beach shack at

Dollarton, British Columbia, experiences recorded in his stories *Hear Us O Lord from Heaven Thy Dwelling Place*, 1961, and his novel, *October Ferry to Gabriola*, 1970. *Under the Volcano* was published in 1947. His *Selected Poems*, edited by Earle Birney, appeared in 1962.

LOWTHER, PAT (1935–75): b. in Vancouver; was co-chairman of The League of Canadian Poets at the time she was murdered in 1975. She had written three books of poems before her death; a fourth collection, *A Stone Diary*, was issued in 1977.

MACEWEN, GWENDOLYN: b. Toronto, 1941; left school to devote herself to a literary career. From 1963 to 1972 she published two novels and a book of short stories as well as writing books of poems. Selected poems old and new, *Magic Animals*, appeared in 1974 and a further volume of selected poems, *Earthlight*, appeared in 1982.

MACINNES, TOM (1867–1951): b. Dresden, Ontario, educated at the University of Toronto; called to the bar, 1893. His *Complete Poems* appeared in 1923 and *In the Old of my Age* in 1947.

MACPHERSON, JAY: b. 1931 in England and educated at Carleton University and at the University of Toronto where she now lectures. *The Boatman* appeared in 1957 and *Welcoming Disaster* in 1974.

MAIR, CHARLES (1838–1927): b. at Lanark, Ontario; educated at Queen's University, Kingston, Ontario. *Dreamland and Other Poems* appeared in 1868, and *Tecumseh: A Drama* in 1886.

MANDEL, ELI: b. 1922 in Estevan, Saskatchewan; educated at the Universities of Saskatchewan and Toronto; at present a professor at York University. Editor and author of many critical literary publications. *Dreaming Backwards*, a selection from his several books of poetry, appeared in 1981.

MARSHALL, TOM: b. 1938 at Niagara Falls; educated at Queen's University where he is now teaching. His cycle of poems organized according to the four elements appeared in separate books and are now gathered in the volume *The Elements*, 1980.

MAYNE, SEYMOUR: b. Montreal, 1944. Has lived in Vancouver and Jerusalem, has taught at the University of British Columbia and is currently at the University of Ottawa. New and selected poems, *The Impossible Promised Land*, appeared in 1981.

MCCRAE, JOHN (1872–1918): b. Guelph, Ontario; educated at the University of Toronto. Served in the South African War and First World War. His *In Flanders Fields* appeared in *Punch*, 8 December 1915, and is the title of his collected poems, 1918.

MCKAY, DON: b. 1942 at Owen Sound, Ontario, attended universities in Ontario and Wales; now teaches in London, Ont. Has published *Air Occupies Space* (1973), *Long Sault* (1975), and recently *Birding, or Desire* (1983).

McLachlan, Alexander (1818–96): b. near Glasgow; came to Ontario in 1840, where he established himself as a farmer, first on his one-acre lot at Erin, and later at Amaranth. *The Poetical Works of Alexander McLachlan* was published in 1900.

McWhirter, George: b. 1939 in Ulster; is a member of the Department of Creative Writing at the University of British Columbia, where he has been managing director of the magazine *Prism International*. He is the author of three books of short stories and several volumes of poetry, the latest being *Fire before Dark*, 1984.

Newlove, John: b. Regina, Saskatchewan, 1938; educated at the university there; has been writer in residence at several Canadian universities. In 1972 his book of poems, *Lies*, won the Governor General's Award; his selected poems, *The Fat Man*, appeared in 1977.

Nowlan, Alden (1933–83): b. Windsor, Nova Scotia; news editor; writer-in-residence at the University of New Brunswick. He authored numerous books of prose and poetry. In 1967 he won the Governor General's Award for his book of poems, *Bread, Wine and Salt*; *I Might Not Tell Everybody This* appeared in 1982.

Ondaatje, Michael: b. 1943 in Colombo, Sri Lanka; educated in Canada at Bishop's University and University of Toronto; presently in the English department of Glendon College, Toronto. His third book of poems, *The Collected Works of Billy the Kid* (1970) won the Governor General's Award; he has written full-length prose works. His poems 1963–78, *There's a Trick with a Knife I'm Learning to Do*, appeared in 1979.

Page, P. K.: b. 1916 in Swanage, England; educated at schools in Winnipeg, Calgary and England. Associated with the *Preview* group of poets in Montreal; has lived abroad and now lives in Victoria, B.C. *Poems Selected and New* appeared in 1974 and *Evening Dance of the Grey Flies* in 1981.

Pickthall, Marjorie (1883–1922): b. Gunnersbury, England; educated at Bishop Strachan School, Toronto. She wrote two novels and a book of short stories, as well as *The Complete Poems* published in 1936.

Pratt, E. J. (1883–1964): b. at Western Bay, Newfoundland; educated at St John's and at the University of Toronto where he taught for many years. The recipient of many honours; three times winner of the Governor General's Award. His *Collected Poems* appeared in 1972.

PURDY, ALFRED: b. 1918 near Wooler, Ontario; attended college in Belleville; world traveller with a home at Ameliasburgh, Ontario. Has published many volumes of prose and poetry, in 1965 winning the Governor General's Award for poetry with *The Cariboo Horses*, and publishing his poems 1958–78 under the title *Being Alive*.

REANEY, JAMES: b. 1926 near Stratford, Ontario, educated at the University of Toronto; professor of English at the University of Western Ontario. One of the leading dramatists in English Canada. *Selected Shorter Poems* and *Selected Longer Poems* appeared 1975/6.

ROBERTS, SIR CHARLES G. D. (1860–1943): b. at Douglas, New Brunswick, educated at the University of New Brunswick. From 1925 on, lived in Toronto. Achieved an international reputation as a poet, and for his nature stories. *Selected Poems* was published in 1955.

ROBERTS, THEODORE GOODRIDGE (1877–1953): b. Fredericton, N.B., brother of Sir Charles G. D. Roberts. Author of a number of romances of adventure. A volume of selected verse, *The Leather Bottle*, was published in 1924.

ROSENBLATT, JOE: b. 1933 at Toronto; now lives at Qualicum Beach in British Columbia. Is well known for his drawings. His book of poems *Top Soil* won the Governor General's Award in 1976; his latest, *The Brides of the Stream*, appeared in 1983.

ROSS, W. W. E. (1894–1966): b. at Peterborough, Ontario; educated at the University of Toronto. Geophysicist with the Agincourt Magnetic Observatory near Toronto. A selection of his poems, *Shapes & Sounds*, was published in 1968.

SANGSTER, CHARLES (1822–93): b. at Kingston, Ontario, where he had his schooling. Entered journalism and then, in 1867, the Civil Service, Ottawa. His collected *Poems* has appeared in the Literature of Canada reprint series. (The stanzas selected from *The St Lawrence and the Saguenay*, 1856, are XI–XIII, XXXI, and LXVI.)

SCOTT, DUNCAN CAMPBELL (1862–1947): b. at Ottawa; educated at Stanstead College, Quebec, and the University of Toronto. Had a long and distinguished career in the Department of Indian Affairs, retiring in 1932. Author of a number of books of poetry and two volumes of short stories. *Selected Poems* appeared in 1936.

SCOTT, FREDERICK GEORGE (1861–1944): b. in Montreal; educated at Bishop's University and King's College, London. From 1925, Archdeacon of Quebec. His *Collected Poems* appeared in 1936.

SCOTT, F. R.: b. 1899 in Quebec City, son of Archdeacon Scott;

educated at Bishop's University, at Oxford, and at McGill where he was Dean of the Faculty of Law. Has written widely on national and international affairs. Co-editor of the anthology, *New Provinces*, 1936, and member of the 'Preview' group of poets in Montreal. *The Collected Poems* was published in 1981.

SERVICE, ROBERT (1874–1958): b. in Preston, England. Service emigrated to Canada in 1894, worked as a bank clerk in British Columbia, was transferred to the Yukon in 1904. *Songs of a Sourdough* appeared in 1907. Editions of his works number in the millions. He retired to France where he died in 1958.

SHEARD, VIRNA (1865?–1943): b. in Cobourg, Ontario; educated there and in Toronto. Author of several books for children. Her selected poems, *Leaves in the Wind*, appeared in 1938.

SKELTON, ROBIN: b. 1925 in Easington, East Yorkshire; educated at Cambridge and at the University of Leeds; joined the University of Victoria, B.C., in 1963, where he was editor of the *Malahat Review* and professor in the Creative Writing Department. Author of many books of criticism and poetry. *The Collected Shorter Poems* appeared in 1977.

SMITH, A. J. M. (1902–80): b. in Montreal; educated at McGill and Edinburgh universities. Taught for many years at Michigan State University. Co-editor of *New Provinces*, 1936, and editor of many anthologies of Canadian prose and poetry. His selected critical essays, *Toward a View of Canadian Letters*, was published in 1973 and his selected poems, *The Classic Shade*, in 1978.

SOLWAY, DAVID: b. Montreal 1941; educated at McGill; teaches poetry at John Abbott College, Montreal. His *Selected Poems* was published in 1982 and a volume of his poems derived from sojourns in Greece, *Stones in Water*, in 1983.

SOUSTER, RAYMOND: b. 1921 in Toronto where he was educated and is an accountant. Was editor of Contact Press and has co-edited several anthologies of Canadian verse. His *Collected Poems* in four volumes appeared from 1980 on.

THOMPSON, JOHN (1938–76): b. in England, educated there and in the United States; was a member of the English Department at Mount Allison University, Sackville, N.B. from 1966 to his early death. *At the Edge of the Chopping There Are No Secrets* appeared in 1973.

VAN TOORN, PETER: b. 1944 in a bunker near The Hague; educated at McGill; has edited several anthologies of Canadian poetry; has played for several group bands. Teaches at John Abbott College in Montreal. *In Guildenstern Country* was published in 1973.

WADDINGTON, MIRIAM: b. 1917 in Winnipeg; educated at the universities of Toronto and Pennsylvania; teaches at York University, Toronto. Editor and author of several critical studies. Poems new and selected appeared in *Driving Home* (1972) and a tenth volume, *The Visitants*, in 1981.

WARR, BERTRAM (1917–43): b. in Toronto; educated there; joined the R.A.F. in 1941 and was killed in action in 1943. Collected poems, *Acknowledgement to Life*, appeared in 1970.

WAYMAN, TOM: b. 1945, Hawkesbury, Ontario; educated at the University of British Columbia and the University of California. Has written several volumes of poetry, *Money and Rain: Tom Wayman Live*, appeared in 1975.

WEBB, PHYLLIS: b. 1927 in Victoria, B.C.; educated at the University of British Columbia and at McGill; lives on the Gulf Islands in British Columbia. Her selected poems, *The Vision Tree*, was published in 1982.

WILKINSON, ANNE (1910–61): b. in Toronto; informally educated, mostly in schools abroad. *The Collected Poems and a Prose Memoir* was published in 1968.

Index of Titles

Index of Authors

MORE ABOUT PENGUINS, PELICANS AND PUFFINS

For further information about books available from Penguins please write to Dept EP, Penguin Books Ltd, Harmondsworth, Middlesex UB7 0DA.

In the U.S.A.: For a complete list of books available from Penguins in the United States write to Dept DG, Penguin Books, 299 Murray Hill Parkway, East Rutherford, New Jersey 07073.

In Canada: For a complete list of books available from Penguins in Canada write to Penguin Books Canada Ltd, 2801 John Street, Markham, Ontario L3R 1B4.

In Australia: For a complete list of books available from Penguins in Australia write to the Marketing Department, Penguin Books Australia Ltd, P.O. Box 257, Ringwood, Victoria 3134.

In New Zealand: For a complete list of books available from Penguins in New Zealand write to the Marketing Department, Penguin Books (N.Z.) Ltd, P.O. Box 4019, Auckland 10.

In India: For a complete list of books available from Penguins in India write to Penguin Overseas Ltd, 706 Eros Apartments, 56 Nehru Place, New Delhi 110019.

Poetry Anthologies in Penguins

A selection

THE PENGUIN BOOK OF GREEK VERSE

Edited by Constantine A. Trypanis

This selection of Greek Verse in the original is the first of its kind to be published in the English-speaking world: it covers approximately three thousand years – from Homer to the twentieth century.

THE PENGUIN BOOK OF ENGLISH VERSE

Edited by John Hayward

A choice of verse reflecting the richness and variety of intellectual and emotional appeal made by the principal poets – some 150 in all – who have written in English throughout the four centuries dividing the first Elizabethan age from the second.

THE PENGUIN BOOK OF IRISH VERSE

Introduced and edited by Brendan Kennelly

Brendan Kennelly explores the origins and development of the Irish poetic tradition, tracing its growth to show its tough capacity for survival despite long silences and methodical oppression and indicating the directions in which he believes it is likely to develop.

THE PENGUIN BOOK OF TURKISH VERSE

Edited by Nermin Menemencioğlu in collaboration with Fahir İz

This anthology is the first published in the English-speaking world to represent the whole span of Turkish Verse from the founding of the Ottoman Empire to the present day.

Canadian Writers in Penguins

ROBERTSON DAVIES

THE REBEL ANGELS

The University of St John and the Holy Ghost (Spook) is jolted out of its crabbed and scholarly pursuits by the return of the evil, brilliant Brother Parlabane, and by the discovery of an unpublished manuscript by Rabelais.

Coincidentally, beautiful, sexy Maria Magdelena Theotky is doing post-graduate work on Rabelais (provoking not entirely academic responses in the breasts of her colleagues) . . . and when the manuscript disappears all the unbridled furies of sex, vanity and violence are let loose.

A glittering extravaganza of wit, scatology, saturnalia, mysticism, and erudite vaudeville, *The Rebel Angels* places Robertson Davies in the fore-front of contemporary writers.

THE DEPTFORD TRILOGY

Who killed Boy Staunton? Around this central mystery is woven a glitter-ing, fantastical trilogy of novels that lure the reader down labyrinthine tunnels of myth, history and magic – exhilarating antidotes to a world where 'the fear and dread and splendour of wonder have been banished'.

Fifth Business

'It has the magic, mystery and irresistible drive of *The French Lieutenant's Woman*' – *The New York Times*

The Manticore

'He is to say the least a mature and wise writer' – Anthony Burgess

World of Wonders

'Fascinating, intelligent and satisfying . . . I couldn't stay away from this novel' – Alan Sillitoe

Canadian Writers in Penguins

ALICE MUNRO

THE BEGGAR MAID

'Wonderful! Whether *The Beggar Maid* is a collection of stories or a new kind of novel I'm not quite sure, but whatever it is, it's wonderful' – John Gardner, author of *Grendel*

As a child Rose had a hard life. Born into the back streets of a small Canadian town, she battled incessantly with her practical and shrewd stepmother, who cowed her with tales of her own past and warnings of the dangerous world outside. But Rose was ambitious – she won a scholarship and left for Toronto where she married Patrick; for him she was his Beggar Maid, 'meek and voluptuous, with her shy white feet', and he was her knight, content to sit and adore her . . .

'A work of great brilliance and depth . . . Munro's power of analysis, of sensations and thoughts, is almost Proustian in its sureness' – Alan Hollinghurst in the *New Statesman*

THE MOONS OF JUPITER

Alice Munro's women discover, in these eleven stories, that love is rarely honest, kind, or reliable (although they keep trying); that people are not puzzles to be 'arbitrarily solved' (although they continue to search the past and present for clues).

Some are beginning new affairs or leaving threadbare marriages; several inhabit that ambiguous time between youth and middle-age. They want 'new definitions of luck' – less to sweep them off their feet than to help make sense of men, families, relationships and life in their contemporary small-town Canada, mapped by Alice Munro with unerring and unforgettable style.

'Alice Munro has been compared with Proust, short-listed for the Booker prize, and remains (though dazzling) quite unperturbed and unaffected, her writing smooth and supple' – *Financial Times*.

Poetry Anthologies in Penguins

A selection

THE PENGUIN BOOK OF LOVE POETRY

Introduced and edited by Jon Stallworthy

Set by theme rather than chronology, Jon Stallworthy's delightful anthology explores men and women's changeless reponses to the changeless changing seasons of their hearts.

A CHOICE OF COMIC AND CURIOUS VERSE

Edited by J. M. Cohen

This volume covers the whole tradition of English and American comic verse writing from the masters – Hood, Lear, Carroll – to the anonymous lampoonists of the eighteenth century, up to the present day.

THE PENGUIN BOOK OF BALLADS

Edited by Geoffrey Grigson

From both Britain and overseas, this rich and colourful selection of traditional and modern ballads includes stories of court, castle and manor, and themes of social injustice, love and war.

THE PENGUIN BOOK OF FIRST WORLD WAR POETRY

Edited by Jon Silkin

In this haunting collection of war poetry, poets who were soldiers are joined by others like Kipling and Hardy who were not combatants yet wrote poetry concerned with the War.